To Ron
with g[...]

The Rendez-Vous

As ever,

Andrew
Paris 2008

ANGLO-AMERIKANISCHE STUDIEN
ANGLO-AMERICAN STUDIES

Herausgegeben von Rüdiger Ahrens und Kevin Cope

Band 21

PETER LANG

Frankfurt am Main · Berlin · Bern · Bruxelles · New York · Oxford · Wien

Andrew Parkin

The Rendez-Vous

Poems of Multicultural Experience

PETER LANG

Europäischer Verlag der Wissenschaften

Bibliographic Information published by Die Deutsche Bibliothek
Die Deutsche Bibliothek lists this publication in the Deutsche Nationalbibliografie; detailed bibliographic data is available in the internet at <http://dnb.ddb.de>.

ISSN 0177-6959
ISBN 3-631-50981-2
US-ISBN 0-8204-6449-X

© Peter Lang GmbH
Europäischer Verlag der Wissenschaften
Frankfurt am Main 2003
All rights reserved.

Printed in Germany 1 2 3 4 6 7

www.peterlang.de

For Françoise

Contents

Acknowledgements

Thanks are due to the editors of the following, where some of these poems appeared for the first time: *Blast [Australia]; B.C. Books [Canada]; The Eclectic Muse [Canada]; The Humanities Bulletin [Chinese University of Hong Kong]; The Humanities Research Centre Bulletin [Australian National University]; Interior Voice [Canada]; The New Orphic Review [Canada]; P.E.N. [Hong Kong]; P.E.N. [London]; Poetry New York [U.S.A.]; Tolo Lights [Hong Kong]; VS: 12 Hong Kong Poets [Hong Kong]; Yuan Yang [Hong Kong].*

Introduction

Our wanderings from our "place of birth" – as passport language has it – make the strange familiar, the familiar strange. We make and keep our rendez-vous with others, or, as many a post-colonial critic would have it, with "the Other".

I've had many such encounters, most memorably ever since I went on a school trip for two weeks when I was fourteen. We went from the "Black Country" and Birmingham (before the Clean Air Act) by rail and sea to Paris. I knew that people supposedly had spoken or still spoke the Latin and the French respectively that I regurgitated in school exercises, parrotings, dictations, and tests. I was nevertheless surprised that the French "others" went around speaking French as if it were the most normal thing in the world.

We "Brummies" were used to grimy Victorian brick buildings, wartime bomb sites growing nettles and hemlock, desolate suburbs of hastily built "pre-fabs", evil-smelling cafés, British Restaurants, and school lunches – called dinners – the only edible course being apple or rhubarb crumble with a glutinous custard topped by a darker skin. Not surprisingly, the splendours and pleasures of Paris delighted me. When I saw the Louvre and Versailles I had an inkling of what our history master meant when he discussed the power of Louis XIV, Richelieu, and Mazarin. I saw the beautiful fantasy of architecture revealed in the Opera Garnier and the façades along the avenues and boulevards. I felt self-consciously young when watched by smiling passers-by as we were lined up in two groups alphabetically to be counted by the two French masters; but I felt very "sophisticated" and part of the scene, when we were all seated on the pavement terrace with *grenadine* or *citron pressé*. The strange gas-filled drink sold next to our school and known to us as "Vimto" was now a thing to be avoided at all costs. Even school milk was no better.

Adults were "other" to "us kids" but there was a strange adolescent apprehension of adulthood when we were taken around Montmartre, Pigalle, and some of the murky streets near the Madeleine. We had been told to say nothing if any "women of the streets" spoke to us. Some of them, obviously amused by a crocodile of young lads, even if we were in long trousers, hissed and called us "chéri" from doorways and court-yards. As we compared notes about this later, some had thought it a great joke to reply to the women with the one English word, "Nothing", thus following to the letter our teachers' instructions. The school trip convinced me to do "A" and "S" level French. It started my life-long compulsion to be in Paris whenever possible. Unlikely as it might seem, perhaps "Baggy" Lindon, the senior French master, is partly responsible for my having married, long after his retirement and demise, a French woman! Or perhaps my francophilia was nurtured early in me by my mother who, although she had to leave school at about the age of four-teen, had started a life-long process of learning French. At ninety-five she had a very large vocabulary and an atrocious French accent. With the aid of her trusty Harraps dictionary, however, she read André Maurois and Colette in the original. She had two brief trips to France, so far as I know, but she would dearly have liked to go there more frequently and mix with people she would never, in those days, have guessed to be oth-ers. Nor would she have been impolite enough to have lumped them all together under such an impersonal label.

Encounters with others through migrations – for a multitude of rea-sons, not the least being natural or man-made catastrophes, trading expe-ditions, holidays abroad, diplomatic postings, troop movements, banish-ment, and exile of all kinds – are as much part of the human experience as settlement, agriculture, villages, towns and cities, people staying put, and their defence by natural and negotiated frontiers, replete with their guards and strongholds. The experiences of wandering and staying at home have been linked historically, of course, by exploration, conquest, and settlement. In recent history, a mere fifty years of the twentieth cen-tury, world population grew in three generations from about two to six billion people, the majority non-white and living in many of the poorest countries. This increasing population has meant also increasing migra-tions to developed parts of the world and therefore increasing encounters with others, whatever race, ethnic group or skin colour they may have. In the same time span there has been increased globalisation, calling in doubt old certainties, cultural givens, personal identities. Nor should we forget the massive urbanisation of former country people crowding the cities, so that we rub shoulders with others whenever we go out. These

16

Greek and Roman culture. Welsh English appeals to me too, as in "The Works", or in older poems like "In Praise of Tenby" or "Among Celts" from my earlier collection, *Dancers in a Web*. In fact, most of us are a rendez-vous of cultures and sub-cultures. The others survive within us. My past is an other. My future is the yet-to-be- encountered other me and you. Within a culture, different regions have circumstances that make them the other within that culture. A wonderful example of how this can be is J.B. Priestley's *English Journey* (1934). In her introduction to the Folio Society's reprint of the 1984 Jubilee edition of the book, Margaret Drabble deftly sets Priestley in the tradition of Dr. Johnson, Cobbett, Disraeli, Mrs. Gaskell and Dickens as travel writers, but she adds:

Priestley strikes many new notes, and this volume helped to open up a new genre of documentary. Part travel book, part autobiography, part investigative journalism, *English Journey* examines working conditions, unemployment, leisure, pleasure, and place. Many of the regions it describes were largely unexplored by literature, and Priestley writes of them with an infectious sense of wonder as well as of disgust. He discovers his own nation at times with the surprised delight of a social anthropologist writing of distant cultures, at times with passionate political indignation.... There is nothing ingratiating about his portrait of the extraordinary ugliness of the 'lop-sided oafs, gnomes, hobgoblins' and the fat, sweating, or 'witch-like, iron-spectacled' women of the whist drive in Birmingham. His harsh comments on the Irish in Liverpool understandably caused an offence which can still be felt today [1997]. He did not write to flatter.

(pp.8-9)

My poems "Slag Fire" and "Exiles" meditate on otherness of different remembered kinds.

The truth of this otherness of one's "own" culture will be recognized by all readers who remember the fragmentary experiences of other times, other countries, other cultures, and their people, that reading makes available to us. We realize that there is more estrangement in ourselves than is dreamt of, even in philosophy.

Our languages contain the residues of previous cultures, many of them foreign. The English language is a supreme example of this. The history of other cultures is on our tongues, even if we do not know it. And the best writing in world literature transcends all nationalities. They speak *to* all of us. They speak *for* all of us. I made the journey to Ravenna, Italy, partly because the Irish poet, Yeats, had done so, partly to see mosaics derived from Greek Byzantium or Constantinople, or Istanbul, city of cultural accumulation if ever there was one, and mainly to see the tomb of Dante, the Florentine, the father of modern Italian, and the world poet no poet can ignore.

The "cultivated" person appreciates the interplay of cultures through language and literature, and their histories, realizing that this interplay is also *internal*, a piece of *cultural* autobiography. In their Preface to *Shakespeare Global/Local: the Hong Kong Imaginary in Transcultural Production* (2002), the editors remark that

> Not only are Shakespeare's characters and stories known to the Chinese as part of the most treasured wealth of world culture, his plays have also become classics of the Chinese theatre, both in the modern and traditional styles. The significance of Shakespeare in Hong Kong and China today can be seen in the fact that the playwright has actually become a site of contestation between the global and the local imaginary in transcultural production.
>
> (Parkin, Tam, and Yip, p.vii)

We post-colonial writers should not forget that Shakespeare himself was a post-Roman-, post-Norman-colonial writer with an Hebraic-Christian education, absorbing and transforming the European others in transcultural ways for local appreciation, understanding, and *misunderstanding* in Elizabethan and Jacobean London.

Language, culture, and their interplay, become a part of the self, that other landscape, a richness given to the living by life, and to life by the living. All of us who use English, whatever our nationality or ethnicity, can ask, with the Welsh poet, Edward Thomas,

Will you choose
Sometimes –
As the winds use
A crack in a wall
Or a drain,
Their joy or their pain
To whistle through –
Choose me,
You English words?

With the development of motion pictures, television, global advertising, and electronic imaging in the last century and this, we can ingest images of alien places, peoples, and their activities. Images of that astonishing natural phenomenon known to foreigners as Ayer's Rock and to Australian aborigines as the sacred Uluru, are flashed around the globe in publicity shots. My "At Uluru" tried to render my experience of seeing it with astonishment for the first time at dawn. When from its summit I saw across the desert a perfectly circular rainbow hovering in mid air in the red distance, I took it for an omen of good will. If no man is an island, no culture, however remote, is an island any more. Those very British games, soccer and rugby football bounce around the world more rapidly than their respective balls bounce from player to player in any match. Even cricket has made a number of very remote boundaries, though there are, we have to admit, certain cultures resistant to the charm of defending three sticks against a hard leather missile with the aid of an elegant willow club. Cultures quickly adopt and adapt what people find to be useful, attractive, amusing, or intriguing, making such elements part of their own resources. Golf is as Scottish as scotch, tennis as French as champagne, and yet these things are embraced by others, become familiar, and are made part of many a different culture.

People who complain of cultures being eroded or overlaid by the silt of other cultures have a real concern, especially when what is loved gets lost and forgotten. Yet history and archaeology demonstrate the demise of cultures every time another ancient site is excavated. Cultural vandals, Oliver Cromwell and the Taliban were no exception, destroy even as they attempt to preserve *their* favoured values. Such vandalism is partly the subject of my "Muse" sequence and also of "Victory at Samothrace". Human beings have infinite capacities, of course, for unreason and hypocrisy.

The poems in this book reflect or embody many of these issues. They were written in and about different places and at and about different times. Just as our personal past can be an other compared to a present self, so history is other. Yet history, like the self, has its continuities and contiguities. Thus the *Official List* I read in the public library in the rue de Picpus in Paris, while here on a trip from Hong Kong, led to my "Official List" poem and made the events of the period of revolutionary terror touch on the terror unleashed by Lenin and later that of the Red Guards and the Gang of Four in China. Meeting Wu Ningkun in Hong Kong after his twenty-eight years of prison camp persecution connected the "Cow Demon" poem with the horrors of la Place du Trône-Renversé (now renamed la Place de la Nation) and with "The Death of Lenin". At the same time, a mature doctoral student in Hong Kong, who had seen the Red Guards at first hand, was writing on Wordsworth with a fresher understanding of his turning away from youthful radicalism after he had been in revolutionary France. A political ideology can be the other, and can have far more scope for murderous terror than the foreigner who happens to be a different colour. Ideologues have a lot to answer for in the story of humanity. Of all the "excuses" for crime, which is always the denial of someone else's rights, ideology, whether religious or political, is probably the most pervasive. To my mind, there is little to choose between the arrogance of class or racial hatreds.

Because the poems in this collection are from different *places* in my life, I have grouped them into sections named by country. The poems, though, may connect in a multicultural way with experience from outside that particular country. "A Portrait of Charles the Bold Found Under a Later Painting" was written and first published and reprinted in Australia but Charles the Bold was Duke of Burgundy and his restorer was a woman with Oxford training living and working in the U.S.A.! The medieval other thus finds its way circuitously into our modernity. Egyptian experience connects with Canada through "Expo 86" held in Vancouver and it was in Canada that I first read and wrote about Flaubert's Egyptian escapade. "Kuchuk Hanem to Gustave Flaubert" was, though, first published in Hong Kong. In that poem I speak with the voice of my imagined "almeh" or dancing-girl/courtesan.

This collection is organized in three parts. In each part there are poems of loss and recovery, thus following the Greek myth of Hades' abduction of his niece, Proserpine, who has to remain with the dead in winter but comes back to earth like flowers in the spring. In each part there are poems of personal experience juxtaposed with poems referring to myth or history. Personal and cultural fractures dominate theme and form in Part III. Vandalism and the mutilations of cultures are balanced by renewal and the discovery of the muses, memory and imagination. My previous collections of poems have used juxtapositions of comparison and contrast like montage in cinematography as a way of arranging and ordering the poems to make a web of interconnections. This collection follows the same principle and procedure.

When I attempt to put my personal and social experience into verse, it seems that my images of a society, its places and situations, derive from my perceptions in a specific place, where I was at the time, and from memories of what once was and of where I once was. The poetry is from the here and now but also from the there and then, the self and the other rubbing shoulders. I am at once at home and in exile. That is the experience of this particular writer. And having said that, I think of the Serbian poet, Desanka Maksimovic, who asserted

But whatever the weather,
for that land where one stays forever
one must set out.

At the same time, I see cultures changing and fracturing. Part Three of this collection, "Shards", tries to render such fragmentation through fragmentary lyrics. It is people themselves, members of societies, who are left to pick up the pieces. In the long run, they usually manage it. Peoples are resilient. I realize, now that I have made this collection, that the connections between the poems in the three parts of the book make, in fact, multicultural connections. Shenzhen, just across the border from Hong Kong, collects fragments of China's ethnic heritages in the park of the 57 cultures, while the university there has a small nuclear physics laboratory. In the park called "window on the world" tourists see a smaller but impressive replica of the Eiffel Tower puncture the sky. In the streets of Shanghai and Souzhou, for example, plane trees flourish, planted to recall the streets of Paris. The Bund, the famous waterfront promenade of pre-revolutionary Shanghai, has now been glitteringly restored and provides the setting for my "Shanghai Woman" who flies like a woman warrior in a Chinese costume movie between the masts on top of the Bank of China building in Hong Kong to her one-time home city of Shanghai, whose dialect she still speaks, although she lives in Hong Kong and has lived in Paris. "When they Killed the City's Dogs" was occasioned by real events in the early days of the People's Republic of China. Nowadays, some Chinese keep dogs as pets. Some features of cultures change, and the changes can be rapid. Others persist, such as the dignitary's privilege of dotting with black paint the eye of the dragon before the celebratory lion dance.

Slang, like a dialect, is the speech of insiders, a shorthand of solidarity. In Her Majesty's Armed Forces "chuffed" means "pleased". A NAAFI break is the desired free time for cups of tea, cigarettes, bacon sandwiches or sausages and baked beans in an informal canteen rather than the "mess", or official dining room. For the new recruit, to be "chuffed to NAAFI breaks" means to be really pleased. This kind of reference is not easily available in the way that Greek, Roman, or other mythologies and histories are from reference books. To some readers, the inkstone may be unfamiliar. It is the carved stone in which Chinese scholars and calligraphers mix their ink with water before writing or painting. These often very beautiful stones can be collectors' treasures.

Another kind of reference in this book is the cross-reference between my previous poems in different publications. An example is that the inkstone is one of the four treasures of Chinese scholars and thus connects with my "Four Treasures" published in *Hong Kong Poems*.

Although my preoccupation with others in this Introduction has been partly autobiographical and experiential rather than theoretical, I am pleased that my plurality of others accords too with the work of academic writers. I refer readers, for instance, to Jacques Derrida's discussions, especially to "Psyché: Invention de l'autre" and to J. Hillis Miller's book, *Others*, where he insists through literary and philosophical commentary on the rich plurality of all that is "others". The others that I seek, encounter, and envisage here exist not as an abstraction but as elusive or familiar features of people, places, languages, dialects, and accents, all offering the possibility of literary consciousness communicating across and within cultures.

PART ONE

BRITAIN

SNOW COUNTRY

This paper with its white depths
leads me into the snow country
where everything but whiteness
lies hidden – no, the black twigs
stand out like a bold hand
in Indian ink.
But somewhere under the drifts
I seek the essence, as yet unknown,
of myself, loving these blunt forms,
frozen waves of land,
and the frost-arrested gestures
of Nature's dead.

THE DUST OF ALL THE YEARS

The dust of all the years
falls silently unnoticed,
until, as thick as fear,
it clouds the mirror
of uncertain emptiness,
recalls dimmed faces from the past
and bears their fingers' traces
and their half-forgotten words.

ON CAME THE TOFF

On came the toff
all black and white
like the Penguin
in *Batman*
and up our street
and down along the cut
we played at him
to take him for real.

He sometimes tippy-toed
on a shiny stage
with a gang of toffs
multiplied in mirrors
and soppy ladies
all our moms wished to be.
In smoky picture palaces
he was debonair Astaire.

He was a real comic too,
staggering drunk as a lord
but never at a loss
to steady the wobbly world,
or himself, with a cane
with a silver knob
as his white scarf
swung loose and hung

long as his tails
and his topper might topple
but never did
when he swung a watch
back into a pocket.

We cheered him on
in the ringed world
of lions and horses
and paid attention
when he cracked his whip
longer by yards
than his waxed moustache.

I like him best
when he pulls doves
from his hat's chimney
and breaks his cane
into a bunch of flowers.

SPITTING ON THE FIRE

Did your dad ever spit
on the fire? Mine did.
Regularly. Each day
after work he would sit,

stare into the flames,
rheumy eyes buoyed above bags
of plump flesh, scheme,
while my toy soldier games

with the chipped army tank
littered the hearth rug
and crawled the black fur
of our dog's warm flank.

Soon he would cough
and the dog stir. He'd
rumble as he hawked
and spat on the tough

coals the juicy grey-green
gob that would sputter
and fizz and dance alive
as heat seared away its sheen.

My clear child throat
constricted and dry,
I tried not to see him,
weary man-whale afloat

in his forbidden chair.
I hated him then.
I couldn't eat at fifteen
if I heard his belch or sneeze
or glimpsed his thin hair.

Now I can see anew that big
smoke-abused body, bandaged leg,
hear him struggle to squeeze
air through frothing lung.
I whiff again the reek
of smoke in the old man's room.
I listen now like a friend
to that rough tongue.

DUDLEY JACK

Only just as tall as us kids
but with miner's muscles,
Dudley Jack, pit-pale,
slouches, one foot turning in
followed by his wall-eyed collie
and, pigeon-toeing it, us kids.

His old suit jacket undone,
greasy cap never straight,
and over the flap
of a collar detached shirt
with never a stud,
the white scarf, undone.

He crabs it uphill to the pub
and after each savage hawk,
wreaking havoc in him,
spits the black gob –
but we follow like pups:
he'll give us crisps at the pub.

How we knew his name we never knew
nor how he got – like a toff –
one of them pilot's white scarves,
when all he did at work
was drop a mile underground in the cage.
When he died we never knew
how we knew – but we knew.

MY APRON

My apron stiffens here and there
with the fat of working days
and gouts of dark, dry blood.

Its blue and white covers my whiter coat,
sleeves blood-stained at the cuffs.
It's no surgeon's kit. I'm just a shop boy.

My hands get greasy, nails tinged black and red,
as I bone out the joints.
I reek marrow and slaughter.

Sheep's head fur gets spiky with blood,
death biting the tongue hard
between grass-green teeth.

I skin skulls, and with my special blade
slice through eyelids, cut out the eyes.
A good cleaver chops straight through to brain.

Two halves of a head lie like deserted nests
on a chopping block scored by blade and bone.
I brush it clean with steel teeth biting wood.

I wipe blood from trays in the window
and wring out the mutton cloth in a pail.
Out front I paint in white: *Hearts For Sale.*

TONG IN CHEEK

It wor in ar back gardin
neeya the chikin coop
amung ar dad's plum trees
all black wi Brummie soot.

Worrow, ar kid! she sez,
Av yow sin *Desoi-er unda the Ellums?*

Ang on a tik, Oi sez, Ooh ar! Oi sin it
last wik but Mick and me went owt
bifo-a where we cum in,
to get the fish an chips loike
an faggits npeaz.

Oh ar, lucky yew, she sez.

Gives me a luk. Yer know!
She puts er coald ands
wun each soide of me faiss.
Oi cud feel er weddingg ringg
freezin on me cheek.
She cum reel close up
and puts er tong in me gob.
It wern't arf warm an good.
Snag waz, it taisted uv Woodboines.

EXILES

Inevitable as the wheat and minerals,
revolution and civil war separated husband
and wife, as they fled their Ukraine.

English as his mother,
he speaks Russian like a boss,
guttural fragments, tongue peeping.

His gunmetal brush-cut head bobs
as he stoops among crab-apples and pears
and wanders through bad harvests of memory.

She trudged across Europe
pawning bits of her jeweled past
to reach English preserves of freedom.

In exile, bitter and sweet
as jam in lemon tea, they begin
all over again, sipping at the future.

She had expected rape –
men are predictable – but she hung on
to her dignity and the mongol child.

One day she shows me her long walk
mapped on the broad soles
of her deep-scarred feet.

She serves me tea from the samovar,
opens banned books with hard signs,
like flags of another history.

In an English back garden
he paints white bands around tree trunks
to keep his fruit insect-free.

When I was ten years old, my gang
stole some unripe pears after dark.
He'd have given us a ripe bucketful.

SLAG FIRE

It smoulders unseen beneath its grit
yet the heap's cone perfects our game –
war of the worlds – and permits the tall-tale smoke
to be volcanic from an island on Mars
near a canal. Wells (H.G.) and Physics
help us shout technicalities of weaponry
and panic like American actors.

Slag fire cat naps under our feet
and we think it reasonably tame.
But when we scratch with heel or stick
it yawns, stretching a flame tongue.
Its red sores fry sausages we prick
with our jack knives, equipped
with a spike to remove stones
from the hooves of horses we whip
by slapping our own backsides.

I pick at the cinder scab,
exposing inflamed insides
of industrial waste that burns,
burns the grown man who never learns
from merciless remains of a past,
that vanished cone, yes, acrid still,
and dumped by the mine we work to the last.

AT A STANDSTILL

Beyond lakes of emptiness
and woods of cunning
at a bend in the road
which passes the asylum
they stand, the quiet ones,
left out like broken tools
in the quarry of silence.

At an edge of the half-truth
of the hospital's vista
a mute harmless one
has reached a standstill.

Look, he has twisted
legs, arms, and wrists,
and even crossed his fingers,
to become his own ivy,
choking the leafless tree of himself.

RIDDLE

The more I am unwound
the more is yet to wind.
My thread's as limitless as mind.
With it every living thing is bound.
Each one finds a start,
each one an end,
yet never knows but one small part
of me, as healer, enemy, and friend.
Although indifferent to every enterprise,
I am the treasure of the wise.

DREAMLAND

Mountains are chisel-toothed
at land's sharpest rim.
Trees grow jagged quills
to prod inky clouds.
The storm tries out its bold signature
across the blank page sky.

Dreamland craves a golden sun
embossed on a blue page.

Above the river's crazed continuo
birds open their beaks
to screech a descant
while the shadows lengthen
in all the secrecy of woods
and the predatory world awakes.

I fear the white moon
embossed on a black page.

At the edge of unfathomed sleep
I'm cornered in a familiar landscape,
where killers track me on the slopes
as I race for the cottage on the hill.
From a window's eye-socket in the wall
I watch as they advance now for the kill.

I observe myself judge distances
and with perfect timing fire my rounds.
My haunted self looks on
seeing the hunters fall
and in the dreamland light lie still.

GET A HAIRCUT

When my hair grows long enough
it starts to make a natural wave
more than a mere cowlick.
Although now gray, the crop's still thick.

At fourteen, dab hand with hair oil and comb,
I'd have mousy locks ruffled by wind
as I biked from school the three miles home,
clocked up by the mile-o at the spokes.

My dad would turn from TV sport or quiz,
eyes blear and rheumy, then ask in general,
Is that lad growing a curl? – and add,
Get it cut, before they take you for a girl.

Later, when I'd proved I was a man
with a new-born son, as strong
as he was long, the old man was glad:
There's nowt o't' simperin' lass about that lad!

He said nothing when my son had long hair.
What would he say, the old man, in his chair,
had he lived to endure son or grandson
with rainbow Huron or cockatoo spikes and tufts?

He would not be chuffed.
He'd fill in "ire" in his crossword
and growl – They can say what they like.
Give me short back and sides any day.

But now he's gone with all good Yorkshire souls
to Heaven's razored lawn and perfect games of bowls.
Time's prize is just a skull, of hair and flesh bereft.
We all grin eyeless with what teeth are left.

CHUFFED TO NAAFI BREAKS

[for Maurice Elliott]

I was chuffed to NAAFI breaks
when you held out your hand.
We shook as if adults,
sucked on our pipes wisely
or flicked oval Turkish cigarettes.

We were randy as only adolescents are
but did what we knew best:
swotting vocab., fooling around,
being irreverent to "The Queen",
saluting with ironic swank
the official enemy's anthem,
thumbing mental noses at some higher rank,
swore at the leaders whose uniform we pressed
and wore, and in which we might have died.

Forty years on, as lovers, husbands, dads,
and grand-dads, genial, irate by turns,
lucky to be here, in fact, we offer thanks,
taking pride in family and friends, and still allow
that love and life are fire – and it burns.

CHANGING TRAINS

The weather, not my marriage, turns out fine.
The joint account is overdrawn again:
I'll leave the train to take another line.

My husband's typist loves to undermine
me – acts the chick, but she's a moulting hen.
The weather, not my marriage, turns out fine.

That man across the aisle seems to combine
the kindness, fun, and charm I need in men:
I'll leave the train to take another line.

Alert, well-travelled, he can read a sign.
His eyes suggest he'll follow me – but then?
The weather, not my marriage, turns out fine.

My husband watches and will soon consign
this rivalry to jokes in a boozers' den!
I'll leave the train to take another line.

We stop. As hubby hunts for food and wine,
my careless love has grasped that moment when
the weather, not my marriage, turns out fine –
we skip the train to take another line.

VYNER'S GIFT

It is the joy, it is the joy I know,
because you nurtured and encouraged, Vy,
and with your gift as boy and man I grow.

The Brontës' moor, a summer's pools, crisp snow
we tunneled through to find more drifts, bright sky:
it is the joy, it is the joy I know.

All ills of war, dead friends, bombardment's glow,
that blackened sky, lost love – I heard you cry –
and with your gift as boy and man I grow.

In wedlock's bitter play you lost a throw.
Society's a mess. Yet still you fly –
it is the joy, it is the joy, I know.

Through ninety years and more you've fooled the crow,
enlivened children's eyes, prized friendship's tie:
and with your gift as boy and man I grow.

Because you live, you love: we reap, you sow.
Then at the last, when you must close your eye,
it is the joy, it is the joy, I know,
and with your gift as boy and man I grow.

THE WORKS

Vera. Vera. Vera!

What is it now, Will?

Vera, I'm going out.

Going out?
You've only just come in!
I just made you a nice cuppa.

I'm going out.

Now now Will, I made you a cuppa.
You've only just come in.

Damn the cuppa. I'm going out.

Oh, language, Will.
What you want to go traipsing up there for?
Cold and wet, it is.
You could be nice and snug yeur
with a cuppa.

Damn the cuppa. I'm going out.

Language. Take your brolly now.

You went up the hill above the works
and me peeking through curtains
of rain pulled across the land,
across the slates and down by the plant.
Day in, day out, like a look-out man.
Now at least you're snug in bed.
You hold my hand now.
Oh my Will, where you going?

DEATH OF A MINOR POET

He made a breathy music
on recorders in his rented rooms
in Cambridge and at Bicester.
I recall his grammar-schooled voice –
Leeds trying to break out –
slightly hoarse and curt,
with a backstreets cunning
in the pale blue eyes
behind the glint of lenses,
as he delivered a devil's chuckle.

He thought to cover with coyness
and brainy talk his disabling shyness
in the company of women.
He grew a blister of arrogance
over his inadequacies,
favouring Nietzsche's superman,
and read the works of Benn
(Gottfried not Tony)
in a secret base
for National Service Russian.

It's what I recalled
when I read that this wiry manikin,
convert to Russian Orthodoxy,
had been casually beaten to death
by a person or persons unknown.
They'd have outnumbered
the little Yorkshireman
hiding behind an ironist's mask.
They'd have thumped him hard
with his own silver-topped cane.

After they left him to die
in the grim streets of his birth,
they'd have spat their way,
swaggering, to yet another pub.

Without the grammar and the poetry,
he might have become one of the boys.

ATROCITY

Too young to be accountable
to any law but hate,
innocent of everything
but a name and a fate,
too young to be accountable,
he hid beneath a table
but he hid too late.

The muzzle briefly rested
in his tousled infant hair.
Dark rose petals spread
on what remained right there.
Do not ask his country.
Do not ask his name.
That he died at all
is every gunman's shame.

SYBIL

Standing on a stone,
she took my adolescent head
between her hands,
stared into my eyes, and said:

You will live without fear of the future.

And I did.

Still on her stone,
she kissed me, lips coral red,
tongue in my mouth,
pushed me away, and said:

You will dream of beautiful, tragic women.

And I did.

I turned and walked away
but paused a moment, looking not back
but straight ahead.
In a strange low voice she said:

You will break a woman's heart.

And I did.

HADES

Can you fathom me?
Under fields lying fallow
I have caves with icy depths.
The water is so clear
you might think it shallow.

The dripping vaults suit me.
With bones I'm perfectly at home
down pot holes in the dark
yet I needed the girl here
deep under loam.

It was easy to bring her down.
She was so intent, my niece,
on picking the flowers
in her mother's meadow.
She begs now for release.

Perhaps I will allow her to go.
I offer the food of the dead.
She takes some fruit and is now my girl
for ever. She sobs for the light,
huddles with fear in my bed.

She's strangely docile sometimes,
giving herself to my gloom.
She will have a share of joy each year,
all that earth can offer, but feel it wither.
That is her doom.

I harvest crops of the recent dead,
prepare her frosty welcome. Call it self-sacrifice
but she is drawn back weeping –
yet not resisting – to my hell.
I will turn her tears to ice.

THE NET

The emptiness around us and within,
sometimes difficult to apprehend
through matter's stubborn presence
and all the circumstances of a life,
waits like an open trap, and so we fall
to voids beneath the scene of mood and thought.

Oh, some, on bold feet, begin,
and then, like dancers, leap and send
expressive gestures of our essence
into the emptiness, sliced by the knife
of their moving shapes, until the call
for the last bow and loss of what they sought.

Others always dither, tremble, delay,
go too gingerly on their way,
imagine not the void but crowding obstacles.
Some offer a high-wire spectacle
and, conscious of the ever-beckoning void,
wield the balancing pole, annoyed
by all distractions. And so we go
taking life's every little blow
or crushing ones.

If we survive
we find time's delicate, tightening net
hanging at the edges of the eyes,
on sagging cheeks, around lips and neck,
holding its catch, older, but still alive.

CANADA

CREATION CLAM

[In memory of Bill Reid]

The great bird, wings spread
in a wild, windy gesture
of vast, sheltering umbrellas
opened somewhere above earth's beach,
grasps in cradling talons
the primeval clam.

The wide arc of the shell's lips,
half-opened serrated mouth,
secretes little men, each with scrotum,
(balls ripening inside like apricots)
scrambling and spilling
in creation's craft.

The ancient image sculpted in blond wood
fascinates the crowds. Bill's vision
shines, impregnates sculpture's history.
Here on Vancouver's Pacific edge,
it's new, unique, and, even cracked, always
imagination's grainy world commanded and commended.

UNSOLICITED GIFT

It turns up one night
in that cold hour before light,
an unfamiliar shape I feel but fail to grip
like some Christmas gift in a pillow-slip,
bulky at the end of the bed.
It fits the heart and head.

A bit the worse for wear,
it's bursting from its wrapping here and there
with not a sign of the return address.
It's truly meant for me I guess.
No hints for care, no use-by-date
but, perishable, it arrives quite late.

With a sudden burst of wit
I somehow get the hang of it.
When it gets turned on
it can play my kind of song.
Can it shoot time's falls
or answer someone else's calls?

I hope that it can know
this moment's gift, just so:
blackbird ranging on the lawn,
wood pigeon's half-completed call at dawn,
bells ringing across the inner court,
the time I spend on books and words I then discard,
the time discerning what I feel and think,
my pencil on the paper near my drink.

NATURE'S BOOK

Nature's book has an invisible source
behind the abundance of whatever is,
all causcs, all results, every elegance
of the measure of matter and force.

Its pages are landscapes and seas,
its book marks fallen branches.
Its fonts are all species
of flora and fauna.

Printer's ink is the rain;
punctuation marks,
asteroids and comets;
textual erasures,
ice ages and floods.

Its words are nature's coinings,
with abbreviations, archaisms
and extinction of the obsolete.
It uses macro- and micro-print.

Sentences and chapters accumulate
but have been edited and cut,
often wrong-headedly, by us.
Our marginalia deface its every page.

Nature's book is a miracle
of literary form, inviting theories.
Though we're just characters in the book
we've learned to read and may even finish it.

Nature's book has an argument
of sublime and microscopic beauty
as well as impeccable, irrefutable logic:
misreading means self-deception.

Like a galaxy of good books from Sunburst Press,
it has an anonymous author, receiving proof.
We don't know why Anon. began it, why still writing,
yet the work pulses on and I don't want to know the end.

ALTER EGOS

Raccoon

It is time for the earth-damp hands
to press apart the green fronds in shadow.
I watch from my fur mask
the world of grass-green grounds
and the pungent sunlit yards,
watch from the fur mask
light falling here in the soft-paced dusk.
And the pungent yards by night
alert my two-tone head
to voices growing in the gemstone dark.
Clawed perceptions sharpened on tree trunks
burrow into my two-tone head
where I face the raccoon self
of clawed perceptions stolen, treasured inside,
finding sense beyond speech.

Heron

This last small fish slides
the length of my slender throat
as I spread my rag wings
to drag my way into vague grey sky,
this stretched feathered frame
with legs atrail, wet from the lake,
flagging myself across grey dusk
as I let fly ahead of me
and of my long shanks, wet from the lake,
from out my chopstick beak,
let fly, fleeting ahead,
yes, one heron cry heard among the trees,
from my chopstick beak
across the tight damp silver fishskin lake
as I descry a raccoon self, spied
from the swaying branch of my destined perch.

NO SECOND ARK

[for Heinz and Gill Kosok]

Sinister clouds in the sky.
Before storm strikes
the first haphazard rain spreads acid
on a garden soon to die.

We have no magic masks or hoods
nor can we lure green gods to love
nor sylvan goddesses to run
ever young in the woods.

We may nevermore laugh or cry
with relief for the ark's returning dove,
a small beak bringing back hope
in a leafy bough, from a rinsed sky.

THE EDGINESS OF BIRDS

They appear sorted into groups,
small condensations of gloom,
in these late days of the year.

They arrive as a handful
flung by the hollow palm
of the big wind, flexing muscles.

Patterned notes on the music paper
wires that squeeze voices
in and out of the telephones,

they seem oblivious yet on edge
as they swoop into the old cedar
and perch, ruffled, on twig feet.

Their companions are nervous squawkers
until one feathery will
huddles them all into a fistful

to deliver a black whistling uppercut
in a long arc across sky's face.
They connect with the big fir

as they glide behind its green brows
in a cloak of invisibility.
It's a bantam weight edginess.

EARTHQUAKE

                    We live on the edge
      of our land-
                        fall craft
ready to spill
mountains sticks and all
into the Pacific

and something beneath soil
      or sea sands
                        crawls
irremediably snaking
                  fault lines of clashing plates
always ready to crash gears

grate together
                        one topping
                              another or
                  depress
disc brakes for the skid
into terror   *terra infirma*
or
            a geological jaw

will open a dark maw
   hungry as pre-history
                        gums agape
mudrims of two worlds

and from wide earth throat
a rumble behind   rockteeth

speaks an ancient tongue
      seismic language
                        of wounds
in the re-opening earth

PRAIRIE FARM

Moving the lines
    crucial as exact words
        men heave   and wheel   the pipes
across fields busy with life

   sky all over enamelled blue   again
      oven left turned right up
         baking the crust of the land
where water hisses steaming across sweat-raised crops

    moving these lines
        whatever else   all day
we snatch a nap under that fierce eye
   of the vandal sun

men have jolted awake
    seen flame bang and bounce
        through crops acrackle
           and roar at the door
                    blistered
and licked black
    by the dry tongues of wheat-gold flames

EGYPTIAN CARVING

In the pavilion we move slowly,
reverently, eager to look and learn,
post-Shelleyan, awed but not overly,
as we inspect the treasure of Rameses,
things lifted from a tomb.

I turn from all the gold
to a small glass case
where the carved girl swims
naked and bold
in our northern air.

She's a mere stick of wood
brittle with centuries;
she cleaves the river's flood
with grained breasts seal-smooth.
She's almost as slim
as a needle of bone.
A typed card says
the duck has gone
on which, once, she rode.

Broken by time,
almost discarded perhaps or missed
by workers with an archaeologist,
she's a snapped bit of wood grain,
trace of a tree once whole.

You have not drowned after all
under waves of indifference.
Slide, little swimmer,
slide like a splinter
through my soul.

KUCHUK HANEM TO GUSTAVE FLAUBERT

1

You call me "star among almehs."
Does that mean you'll pay –
oh yes, I'll settle – more than for others?
Shall I be your pet lamb,
my wool yellow with henna?
I'll use only this tongue
to repay indignities,
this tongue you made a fetish.
My kisses smack of luxury.
You wield a tongue
agile with foreign words.
You trace your image
in the mirror of my race.

Your eyes gleam with curious desire.
I know those oblique glances.
You mount after your friend,
almost like a rape,
your fantasies about to come true
in the reality of white flesh
slaking its thirst
with dark Damascus coffee.

I think in your deepest kiss,
your tightest embrace,
your hardest thrust,
you ache for an ideal love.
You shake with some guilt of Europe.

In the scent of roses
warm from my breasts,
I see you still,
my necklace of gold coins
between your teeth, as you spend,
as you stare in my eyes,
as you growl like a tiger.

2

You leave behind
"the melancholy of steamers"
unpredictable awakenings,
the shock of strange landscapes
and their ruined friendships.

DREAMERS

All of us are there
with Chekhov's company
of idle, smiling dreamers.

Our table's a moon disc
ringed by garden chairs.
A vast umbrella spreads
its dark stain.

A basilisk lurks
in the melancholy mood
to still our laughter.

The white, flustered bird
palpitates and stares
with its girl's eyes.

The girl glides for the shadow
as a Russian dancer would,
one arm raised and bent
across her feathered brow.

Oh heart, nest in the fibres
of youth's ravaged wood.

TRANSPACIFIC

[for Michael Bullock]

A snow leopard springs
from cloudy veils of Chinese hills
front paws on ground zero in Japan

tail in a taut curve to sweep
across the Golden Temple
with its liquid self-reflection

another bound and it's here
under the rainbow arc
from Totem Park to Howe Sound

crouched behind bamboo clumps
in your West Point Grey yard
and whirls round to become you

your eyes are still shining
above that wizard's beard
and the snow on its fur

is your wild hair with its tail
and its dream changes its spots
into your childhood terrors

yet perhaps you will change again
to fly to the great roc's nest
or like Merlin invent Geoffrey of Monmouth

to tell your stories breathed through shell lips
of cowries under waves before you sleep
in a sable womb beneath Stonehenge.

ON THE WINGS OF THE BLACK SWAN

[for Michael Bullock]

You roam across fantastic landscapes
in pursuit of a dark goddess
and a woman from the great lake at Wuhan.

Nature in her many guises
never fails to offer rough nipples
to feed your hungry lips.

Your hydrogen thoughts
are compressed with feelings of sulphur
and your fingers leak acid.

You have climbed a mountain
to engrave on a rock face
a different logic, another wisdom.

In your doctor's office
an ultrasound image of your heart
reveals that it, too, is engraved:

a dark woman caresses your face
as she embraces a black swan.
You make love to her

as if you held a younger planet in your arms.

TWO REALITIES

The prince who finds the rock,
slaughters the monster,
sets free the chained girl
and prises open a new world,
taking the almond from its pitted shell,
has also broken a vow,
and left behind a home,
a weeping wife,
a bewildered child.

DAEDALUS DREAMS OF ICARUS

I land in the shallows
on salt sands of the shore.
The water's dimples
shine each with its star.

My boy falls wingless
from the sky's enamel:
next day I find weed
wrapping a foot and ankle.

With desperate shouts
I plunge into waves,
and sweating in the sea,
hold tight the son my dream saves.

Clutching my child, his severed foot,
I race for shore again.
I have known all the panic of loss,
all the terror of his pain.

As I wake, he vanishes,
the pale dream child in my arms.
He was made whole once more
and safe from life's alarms.

He's dream-safe as anyone can be.
Reality swarms back until the next dream time
in or out of the labyrinth
and that monstrous, sacrificial crime.

KIDS LIKE CLOWNS

[for Ben and Jenny]

Kids like clowns to run tumbling in the ring
loving their own crazed sawdust gags,
hoarse hoopla as they squirt water
unrepentant and irreverent
when a straight man tries to sing
or play Pagliacci
on a fiddle with one string.

White starred eyes, red ping pong nose,
the tonsured wig, the flapping shoes,
and clothes too big – kids want them to remain
eternally the same. They don't value
that melancholy the adult knows
behind grease-painted joy.
Their delight is riot, tumult, in the shows.

And smaller ones who watched a show
with open mouths, surprised by laughs,
or suddenly afraid of the grotesque,
go home reluctantly, if ratchety and tired,
wanting ever more from clowns, who blow
immense balloons, produce more tricks,
more knockabout, the zany and its after-glow.

And when, at home, at last,
the children fall asleep,
we watch the heavy eyelids close,
forgetful of the mischief and misrule,
and marvel at the beauty of the face unmasked
by sleep, and fragrant, as we bend to kiss good night,
oh delicately tinted, like an early rose.

MIND MUSIC

[for Rüdiger and Uta Ahrens]

The mind has its own music,
monotonous percussion of the commonplace,
not so often the whisper of a stream,
more the clinking of a train on cliché's rails,
its note changed by switch points
of unanticipated interrupting notions,
before bookish motifs sidle in like woodwind
and develop with the bowing insistence
of contingent strings of memory –
memory – whose repetitive penetration
surges up from depths of being,
conspires to accompany moments,
trumpeted and brazen, of decision
or glissandos into indecision –
yet I detect at unselected intervals
something precious, a motif I follow
until a melody arrives, a fluent melody,
held by my clarinet of dream
in an improvisation of the soul
and then astonishing rubato, and a crystal descant
of revelation, all disbelief in counterpoint!
The mind has a music of its own.

A MODEL FOR MAGRITTE'S 'BLANK SIGNATURE'

1

Many a time she has sprawled naked
on the studio's lumpy couch.

This time, as paint dries,
she sits straight and demure
in riding habit and boots.

She will trot the great mare
keeping to the thread
(not a difficult crossing)

of dignity stitched into the impossible wood
of the stretched imagination
on his fibrous canvas.

This, once perceived,
makes gallery glancers pause.

2

Why should she not sprawl naked
on the studio couch
and as the painted image dries
mount, as form and colour fit,
to tread on that fastidious mare
the tranquil thread of dignity
woven into the wood's mysteries,
soft night gathering
among her trees?

3

Sometimes he would find her already naked,
stretched on his austere couch.
She would anticipate wrongly his intent.

She looks through the window at infinity
as he integrates incongruities
to deliver a painterly surprise.

Form and colour call for her,
mounted, as her slender image dries,
to post on the elegant mare.

She rides along those fibres of dignity
in a surreal wood never seen but here
or known, even by the old Douanier.

No startled jungle beasts
stare from a lush lair,
a wood dense as animal mind.

All woods are cunning with rustling mysteries.

MODELS

[for Margaret Davis]

Wide-eyed with masks of petulant gloom
or   teeth clenched in smiles, slick models   strut the ramp
elbows bent   a foot out turned   hip jutted
for the hiatus   high fashion's pose   the glossy   still
where lustrous lips   or eyes   or fan-blown hair
conspire now with sun-filled lamps   with bone and flesh
to fit sartorial contrivances to lure us
and then catch applause
or frisson of surprise   for canny lens

and spinning
for the flair of coat   or skirt
on needle   heels   stern mandrels
for floating arabesques of cloth   arch looks
their contortions' weave
ragtrade's mystique:

girls prized for height and bone's slow
guile   to mould a neck   dispose the eyes
stretch the skin to some exotic show
seen in dreams of merchants   fantasy for sale
flounce and flaunt and stroll
vanish

to fret and sweat   behind black drapes
while they change their costumes for a wearier flesh.

COMMERCIAL BREAK

Authoritative hands clap.
Heads hanging, dancers rest, hands on knees,
and their small breasts rise and fall.
Lungs greedy for breath, their high energy's spent
in the choreography of SELL!

Stellar's jays, galahs, sulphur-crested cockatoos,
parakeets of any torrid hue,
the dancers palpitate and gulp
sweat-odour air through open mouths.

Off camera, one dancer sucks at a water bottle,
another smokes away at chances of a longer life,
a third, thoughtful, towels sweat,
listens to another read out tid-bits
in an airmail from a friend.

Video replay, please!
Amazon rhythm spills energy back
into the panting originals
from their screened images
and the throbbing beat.

Music and dance already taped
are on the instant beamed abroad
and into space forever.
These imaged ones are models now
for other girls trying not to be ignored.

At once the dancers lure the window shoppers,
embody ancient lore in modern womanhood.
These laughing girls are yet inside my head
and do not dream of being wife or mistress
to that love-sick boy, Narcissus.

WINDOW DRESSING FOR THE FALL

Snow-capped Mount Fuji
sprayed on the back wall
looms behind mannequins
planted on a fake beach
in or out of bikinis:

Printed skins of lizard, snake, or leopard sprout
hieratic gestures of brown plastic limbs.

Wigs black, blonde, and silver ash
gleam under track lights.
One paper parasol like a huge sun
peeps over an indifferent shoulder.
Fuji yawns as a door opens in the cone.

Enter busy man in socks.
He unties bikinis, casually collects wigs.

Mouth clamped on pins
he re-enters the sacred mount.
Then he's back in the window
unhitching arms and legs,
unplugging a few bald heads.

Distorted limbs await gloves and hose
and looking askance, heads their hats.

A hand, an arm, 'braceleted and bare' signal
from a mound of nylon grass. Design's mad butcher
performs a season's carnage
in the hiatus between summer and fall
for sacred fashion's sake.

ANOTHER MODERNITY

[for Laura Wee Lay Laq]

In the forest you search
for that clay you need
and these particular woods
for firing the pots.

In the forest you keep watch
for required forms coiled
in the silence of your mind.
Because you sit quiet and still
for invisible hours, animals and birds
find no fear around you.

You speak with curved vessels,
their clay shaped by hands and eyes,
then smoothed by rock hard discipline
of the grip of preferred stones.

Shapes you sculpt and fire
crowd imagination's glowing kiln.
On a shelf or a table in a home
in New York, Vancouver, Paris, or Hong Kong,
their elegance commands attention,
like a theorem you figured in the forest's clay.

Your methods are as old
as people in times
beyond history's reach.
Craft's continuities endure.

THE FAMILIAR SUDDENLY IS CHANGED

[for Keith Alldritt and Joan Hardwick]

The familiar suddenly is changed.
Because she once was there,
the corner shop, the pub,
the quiet house re-opened
for the holidays and books,
frosted pavements underfoot,
suddenly were real and beautiful,
like the warmth in her coat
when you walked arm in arm
in breath-corroding winter.

Once, when she was there,
I came round for dinner,
hiding shyness, perhaps,
and awkward in the knowledge
of her impossible illness.
As she laughed and then hugged
all standard words fled
and I felt crass.
It was a matter of glances and smiles.
I don't know why, but I called her "lass".

It was then I knew
all the centuries of tenderness
in one word
because she once was there,
merry as an elf,
in spite of the grimmest burden,
in spite of the limits
of her time as herself,
a little time to spend
with family and friends.

In her absence, somehow, she's within.
She is still on your side.
Her voice and words nest
in particular books, in her notes.
Even I, just a friend, see her again
when I say to myself, "lass",
because she once was there,
although she is no more,
standing in the little hall,
knowing full well the score.

WEST COAST TANKA

Wind-race mountain slopes.
Purple-faced azaleas
wave to the tired sun.
Cloud obscures his concentrate
of fire, silvers the huge mask.

NEW BABY

I relish the true gaze
of the new baby girl,
a child's free stare
frank, almost mystical,
coming from somewhere
still unknown and unforeseen,
the eyes so clear...
they know so little now
not even fear...
some milky trouble
will bring the creasing face,
the crying out for comfort
or the tear...
and sudden weariness unplanned
will close the delicate eyelids
on the world we've made.

UNPACKING

While you are making our improvised lunch
I unpack another box
and discover suddenly remembered odds and ends
from another half-forgotten life.
Crumpled newsprint wraps with frantic
or scandalous stories a Chinese bowl.
Old news signals me with crises
now inconsequential as any wrap and pad.
In the potter's blue and white
there are dried roses I remember
from when you put them there –
was it a decade ago? –
Smiling, I almost weep for our younger selves.
"It's ready!" Your voice is just the same.

CHINA

HONG KONG CROWDS

[for Arthur and Diana Li]

Pell mell crowds in traffic noise and fumes
assault the length of Nathan Road.
In the trees' or tenements' shade
from Tsim Sha Tsui to Sham Shui Po
the crowds parade the length of Nathan Road.

In the dense throng of countless genes,
each bearing a hidden human load
of past, of present, future, there,
what talents, what inventiveness
rub shoulders as they wait fruition?

Who jostles others in the gauntlet run
of market-threshing Mong Kok crowds?
Each spiral of success sprang from encoded
histories of energy where the Pearl River flows.
What talents grow in tenements and villages?

On Sundays, Filipina maids flock in force
to make a female festival of cards and chat,
where in the week the cars kept running or were towed.
Maids squat on stools along the length of Battery Path
for grooming of their hands, their heads, their spreading toes.

In the humidity's rank embrace
they ignore time's copy watch and quartz,
ignore adjacent, urgent crowds,
and picnic out of plastic bowls
near the *tai tai* shops' displays of Spode.

How can we here and now inspire and groom
the overwhelming, fretting crowds
with a brand new deal, another hand,
never knowing all the cards,
in lives as long or short as our genetic code?

THE EVACUATION OF KOWLOON CITY

It's a poisonous little cyst.
It needs civic surgery.

At last, after riots,
the Red Guards,
the Gang of Four,
the laying of the hungry ghosts
of Marx, Lenin, and Mao,
and after the accord
in the rosy dawn
of one country, two systems,
after Tiananmen,
after the restoration of confidence,
and the destruction of confidence,
an intervention in Kowloon is permitted
to remove malign growth.

Infirm shops stock ancient medicines,
dentists put a client's savings
into gold caps, perhaps,
soothsayers bluff the future,
and politicised thugs are bluffed by the future.
All inhabit the rotting tenements,
rising levels of hope and despair
street above street,
and breathe the stink of human evacuation.

Some fight to stay with the rats
infesting a medieval place.
They want none of our modern bait.
They are pre-modern. They like it that way.

Kowloon City!
Just the sound of its name
makes me shed the years,
like an old shirt.

I'm back there as it was
in the riot-tested sixties.

When we arrived at the wall
we showed ourselves at the grill
then passed through a narrow doorway
into the squalor of another dynasty.

Followed by toughs at every step
along stepping stones or paths
above middens and open sewers
we found the old man
with concave cheeks
lying quietly as always
on his board bed
in a dark corner,
patient in death's waiting-room.

His wife offered tea.
The social worker said,
'Accept – but you don't have to drink.'

The grand-daughter slept
in a cardboard box
impervious to the roar of jets
at a hundred feet.

Now I see on a friend's videotape
just the dripping alleys,
power lines of the exposed present
in great swathes and ganglions,
as if some leprous hide were peeled away
from a varicose tangle of veins.

Rain taps out its code from the past
and a random fit of coughing
shoves me back again to that man who dies
in a little cubicle of dark.

Note: Kowloon City, a walled area of Kowloon, was not leased to the British and remained outside the control of the Hong Kong government until not long before the handing back of the New Territories to China in July, 1997. It has now been evacuated, demolished and redeveloped.

XI WANG MU

You left the Palace of the Jasper Pool,
came down from the Kunlun Mountains
and appeared to me at the cross roads
hard by the salt lanes of the sea.

Intent on your best hidden purpose,
you spared a moment to take my arm
and turn me back to the true way,
Queen Mother of the West.

But how will I know to follow
the twists and turns of the true way?

BIRD'S EGG

We have slept under the velvet
of tropic nights for many years
and walked, hand in hand, through the groves
of bananas and silver-green bamboo
along the trails of volcanic islands.

We have explored earth's
geological stretch marks
and have been awakened by storms
cracking open the sea-drenched shell
of the oyster sky.

We have made love in the long afternoons,
clamorous with cicadas,
when happiness surprised us
like the small, colour-splashed shell
of the warm egg of a rare bird.

WHEN THEY KILLED THE CITY'S DOGS

[for Göran Malmqvist]

They did it to protect the public health.
The word *dog* disappeared from readers.
In the head there remain the howls,
especially of the first dogs to die.

I cycle, airedale trotting alongside,
on a certain day and date,
my dog allowed, concession to a foreigner
working in an embassy.

The state's eager children read
See the man cycle.
He cycles from birth to death.
Can the ... run?
The ... can run.

Children run beside my shining spokes
shouting the names of likely beasts
like *Lion! Lion!* At my dog,
the word for which is now
not theirs to know.
The ... name is Rover.
See Rover run.

Cries of the children fade.
My airedale lopes along
caged in blanked minds of the young.

I thought it chic to call him simply Dog.
I wish I'd named him.
There are those who remember
the howls of the last dog dying.

A COW DEMON STUMBLES INTO THE LAND OF PEACH BLOSSOM

[for Wu Ningkun and Li Yikai]

I rinse an old pot I find
at the back of my flea-market mind.
What's this? Nostalgia for an orchard,
its humpback wall, peach trees in bloom?
Just images in cracked glaze.

Youths have hung a label around my neck:
Cow Demon, it reads. I lacked respect.
With fist and foot they teach us antithetical abuse!
They give us feed, hard labour, and correct our thought
to satisfy all social need and use.

Peach blossoms gleam on a broken pot
I scour in the mind's stream.

Under my bed's stained mat
Du Fu and Shakespeare are nibbled by a rat.
Denmark's a prison! I shout in the yard
or when digging another's grave.
Ironies for an uncomprehending guard.

My family's denied a Maoist bliss
in exile even more remote than this,
but I no longer weep and groan at night
for the children and wife I miss.
I hear the crash of falling peach trees!

Despite exhaustion and our cries for grain,
constant revolution has no need but pain.
From my cowed head sweat drips and runs.
One man wipes his brow with soil-caked hands
and toothless, still defiant, tells us all:

This is today; yet there will come another time,
when kids sell peaches from the market stalls.

Peach blossoms fall on that broken pot
I scour in the mind's chill stream!

[Note: In Chinese tradition the Land of Peach Blossom suggests an ideal country, while cow-headed demons lead people astray. 'Cow demon' became a term of abuse used by Maoist Red Guards against victims such as old academics and free thinkers during the so-called 'cultural revolution'. Wu and Li recorded their sufferings in *A Single Tear.*]

WHITE BIRD

White bird winging from the sea at dusk,
you nest beneath those great torn leaves
where the green fruit hangs.

There is a white bird
gliding through my mind.
It cries just once at dusk,
a cry to spear the heart,
as if its mate were lost.

White bird, white bird,
your nest is here,
entangled in our flesh and blood.

When it departs again,
beating through cold air of the waning year,
and, silhouetted in the sky,
flies above village roofs
across the legislature's dome,
circles city banks,
and mounts beyond the hills,
we are left cursing in the traffic's snarls,
uncertain of the problems that we face,
not knowing what we are, and may become.

White bird, white bird,
with the slow beat of your wings
come back to us in Spring!

Glide calmly home
through smoke-yellowed light
across the hillside graves.
Flex your wings above the tangled leaves
and settle like hope within that flimsy nest.

MOUNT O-MEI

[for Michael and Khuan Sullivan]

The pilgrims are immobilized by distance
as they climb the staggering pathways
up the rocky face, moth-browed, silent poetry
of sun shot silk across the sky's old slab.

The gate-house through which all must pass
above Ox Heart Rock vibrates in the sun
and the mountains crane their necks
and cast shadows long as antiquity.

Old women carry life-hoards of tattered notes
as they labour towards the one long-imagined
corner of an enduring world of river and flood.
Along the Yangtze gorge echo the gong and drum.

Clouds stanch the bloodseep wound of the sun
re-opened at dawn. Clouds wipe the sky's blue slate.
The old ruminate on distance and lives dwarfed
as they rest on a climb to eleven thousand feet.

Grannies, some losing their lank hair, arrive,
their chatter festive, breaking the tedium
of an average life. Lovers hold hands.
A light breeze shakes holy lamps on junipers.

At the summit, sound of a bronze bell.
A cloud opens its rainbow lashed eyelid.
Green gaze of the quiet earth eye
at Buddha's perfect emptiness and glory.

A silent youth, poised on the rampart,
dives, bathed in universal light,
He aims for the celestial O,
eager to ride the rapids of the air.

As he falls, turning over
like washing in a dryer,
he tries to look straight in the eye
his jade green Nirvana.

OLD MOTHER

The old woman sits quietly thinking.
Eyes half-amused, it seems,
gaze into a now silent past
away from the din and bustle
of this shuttling train
headlong as thought itself.

Her eyes return to now,
she raises her arm and nods,
beckons with big-veined hand,
green bangled wrist, for me to take her seat.
I hesitate but she nods, insists,
and I realize she'll be getting out.

I slide onto the still warm seat
and already she has vanished
among a shuffling multitude.
In my swaying world
she is the long train of memory,
mothering the here and then.

This remains: her eyes meeting mine
across the clamorous aisle
of the subway train –
her memory is the fantastic landscape
of that far country
nothing can defile.

I imagine her daughters
eternally young, joining past to present,
weaving the never-ending threads
and beckoning like her
as I will beckon others to take my place
and contemplate whatever's still to come.

TANKAS FOR HONG KONG HARBOUR

1

Voices of water
speak from your depths the last words
of Keats, repeating
lines from his little room
bubbling with thoughts of Du Fu.

2

Light on sea ripples,
dance your dance of reflection
of salt water moods
in restless years of exile,
in the furrows of my brow.

VOICES OF THE PEOPLE

Voices of unwritten ones,
hoarse with the cries of work
and the hawking of wares new or old
lugged about in tricolor bags,
call from the dying depths of sea lanes,
shout through the fumes of traffic!

In the glint of polluted waves,
yell salt words of history's mood
to pierce air's ear, higher than kites.

From buses and trams, trucks and vans,

bellow with voices strained
and vocal cords thick as ferry ropes
frayed by the weight of the people!

Chant to guard what is already made good.
Chant to defend spaces and freedoms from blind planners.
Chant to fulfil human needs amid broken promises.

Never forget the generations of hate.
Always forgive the loves of the young!

TOLO LIGHTS

I sit at my desk this long, sleepless night
and gaze at the scene below:
Tolo Harbour, waters blacked out of sight –
but three small fishing boats I guess
shed a steady lure of light.

Traffic to and from Tai Po
still streaks the long pelican beak of sea
edged by tall lamps with orange glow,
spreading like a stain on glass
near traffic's endless flow.

Colour skids in the wavelet's dent,
marbles each smudged spark,
and spills over the sea's bent
lower mark, as over some sleek fall,
and then, at last, is spent.

And I am lost to the city's urgent pace.
Feeling an older beat, not knowing why,
I gaze at the half-hidden face
of the rounding moon, old gate through the night
to love, still sleeping, unconscious of her grace.

Moon, quicksilvering the sea,
silver now the indifference of space.

IN THE FORUM AT THE CHINESE UNIVERSITY OF HONG KONG

In the shadow of white stone
and climbing silent columns
colours signal the brief life
of petals vivid as girls
surrounding the butterfly brides.

Fish, fluid as mercury,
slink through thought's shallow pool.

On the stone seat
old couples doze in the sun.

The scent of roses
haunts their dreams
like favoured daughters
who were lost
and then returned.

DYNAMITE

Another sunset blooms to fade,
a sudden crescent moon has climbed,
a last black butterfly meanders by
like some lone drunkard's shade –
and then we hear beyond the hills
the muffled thuds of dynamite.

Controlled explosions of the rocks
slice the mountains near Shenzen.
Macrosurgery leaves sheer cliff scar
and land remodelled for the docks
where neither charm nor mystery remain.
Engines growl bass burdens to our song.

No pavilion sits as if afloat on mountain mists.
No boom of distant waterfalls. No scholar-poets
share a jug of wine and ponder
every mystery that still exists
or listen to a bamboo flute
until the mind's a blank at last.

Imperatives of change decree the lines of trucks,
equipment bigger than a house, swarms of dusty hardhats,
dredgers, turquoise sea made brown and grey,
the bucking sampan where a fishwife chucks
dead fish back into the oily sway.
Yachtsmen sail in and turn about.

Container ships drop anchors in a floating queue,
decree another terminal
that cannot be contained
and can never be the last.
Vanished hills once made a view.
Red characters proclaim development as progress.
The picturesque is blasted into landfill.

CHINESE RENAISSANCE

Old men lugged their power
as they staggered to the grave.
They abandoned Marx and Lenin
for there's little there to crave.

Now here's youth, impatient,
Knocking, knocking on the doors:

Give us a Chinese Renaissance
of wealth, not Europe's old ideas,
for gold's the one reward
for blood, and sweat, and tears!

Arthritic knuckles whiten
on the handle of a stick;
but that Renaissance of wealth
will make the cities slick.

Yes, it's youth, impatient,
Knocking, knocking on the doors:

There's a need to swagger
on the big world stage,
a need that's far more pressing
than ideologies and rage.

While the images of Chairman Mao
are trinkets you can trade,
still some old ones clutch at power
till the urn's set in a grave.

And it's youth, impatient,
Knocking, knocking down all doors.

COAST ROAD NEAR KAOHSIUNG

In one sunflecked instant
there mounts from the ninth wave
a green birth membrane
of cowlick water ashine.

It ruptures into an open-palm
smack of water in turmoil on sand
and from its clouded shallows
a goddess of the sea arises dripping pearls
between what's yet to come
and China's tragic history.

THE BIGGEST BUDDHA

There he sits above the chatter
of humanity, the biggest Buddha,
and gazes towards China
from the convex surface of his eyes.

Climbers from the monastery
are strung on the ridge
amid unravelling clouds,
beads from a broken rosary.

The shrine's incense coils smoke in air
where the cones, the spirals, glow of gold,
the humble gifts of fruit
are stubborn realities amid muttered prayer

and all the uncertainties we share.

The bundle of written sticks offers
like a city crowd of many different fates,
serene yet unpredictable characters,
or lives shaken by love, or the cruel, or the proud.

The biggest Buddha absorbs the heat
of day and tropic night,
talisman of a star-torn sky,
flung towards China's might.

Beads from a rosary are seeds of light.

INKSTONE

It has sides
straight and small,
a quarried beauty

with carved face
of stone, purplish
forehead, long lips, the one eye.

Stone severities
tooled smooth for ink
trap water and cloud.

Thought's severities
issue in soft brush strokes,
call to writer and reader,

call from ink and stone
paper or scroll
through the centuries

and then recall
each hand, its poetic character,
against life's impatient scrawl.

PINE PLUM AND CRANE

(for Jakuchu who painted them)

A loaded brush brings sky's dull pane
alive with the pine's crooked wires.

How can this other bent bough
bring not barbs but blooms and flesh of plum?

What answer could exist outside the scroll?

Nothing at the time halted
the artist's mystery of growth.

Unerring from broken egg to great oval void.
Foreground feather-fringed

small head, long beak
balanced plumb above bird bulk

and one ringed eye
a gun barrel's end

hides among feathers
and is trained on human dynasties.

MOORED AT THE MAPLE BRIDGE AT NIGHT

Moon going down
and the crow's complaint
on frosty air blown
over maple-lined waters' flow.
Heavy with sorrow
and the sleepless night
spent staring at the boatman's light.
Han Shan Temple outside town
and ringing of its midnight bell
reaching us, where we moored our craft.

Note: This famous poem by Zhang Ji, cut in stone at Cold Mountain Temple, Suzhou, was translated by Wang Yao-han in Suzhou and revised by Andrew Parkin in July 1992. It was a response to adversity, written after the Chinese poet learned he had failed an important imperial examination.

NEAR BRIDE'S FALL

Along the path, the heong tree waits
agitated by a northern breeze.
She wears green hair elaborately teased
and bright with kingfishers.
A girl preparing for a special date,
she breathes her sweet perfume.

Dark clouds are watch towers
on the mountain range.
A wind like some old servant comes
bustling back, rustling with rumours
of the needy, older groom
with flooded fields, way beyond Lo Wu.

A thousand insects wind and then unwind
their ratchet clockwork
as if time itself ran fast
beside the white fall's wedding veil.
And then a slow, fat rain begins.
It flecks the worn, veined stepping stones.

The late hour weeps like a mother for her girl.

Note: The heong or hong tree has aromatic wood used in the manufacture
of some incense or joss sticks. It was shipped to Southern China and thus
gave its name to Hong Kong (Fragrant Harbour).

HAPPY HOUR IN HONG KONG

The singers, two bamboo beauties,
taking turns caress the mike,
sound perfectly American,
their phrasing 'very Peggy Lee.'

Between the sets they speak
with the accents of Manila streets.
Back at the mike again
they snap ringed fingers to syncopated beats.

They open wide their painted lips
to release from gold encircled throats
the high notes and the blue
they've learned by rote.

And yet there's more:
the pleasure that they take
in rhythm, melody, and words,
vitality that spills beyond mere fake.

Americans may think of other happy hours,
interrupt the chat, and drink, and pause,
remember home in Oakland or New York,
and as they listen, offer their applause.

And even I, Canadian by choice,
familiar with quarter, nickel, loon or dime,
recall the voices in Vancouver, Montreal:
'Oh baby, do it to me one more time...
Yeah, baby, do it to me one more time!'

IN THE EYE OF THE LION

Lion, old hollow head,
with iridescent river of a body
in silks that writhe and spread
across villages and the shaded court
where glazed tiles decorate
overhanging curves of roofs,
your feet stamp a parody of lions
across any old street
to sway towards another temple door
and leap to snap at the high lettuces
of some new economic feat.

I

must now
prime
the
brush

approach your huge cocked head
and with a flourish to set all dancing

careening and preening
stepping and stamping
swelling and billowing
involuntarily
a tumultuous tormented sea
of brave waves
and drums, gongs, cymbals,
where all with their colours fly

I

will suddenly dot
one great ping-pong
hovering
wobbling
ogling
eye.

Yes, look, this lion dances
and will again
though others die.

HILLSIDE GRAVE

Behind squat doors where hope lies stilled,
the dead are bones and dreamless dust.
These Chinese ancestors have closed their eyes
on nonchalant slappings of the tides
and found oblivion where wild flowers thrive.

And yet some undercurrent of my mind
insists that spirit may endure,
that even now, it hears with me,
as darkness blots the end of day,
the cuckoo's cry and insects ticking night away.

Huge storm clouds gather in oppressive heat
and then the sky is ripped by light.
The spirit's plaint is lost in thunder claps
crackling through the dusk, across the creaking sampans
in the bay, lamps swinging in and out of view.

Yesterday a last grandchild swept the grave
and burned a paper dollar for every dollar
of the exile's fare he saved,
leaving the village to its damp decay.
The living came, and wept, and showed respect.

This patch of burnt, damp soil amid the grass
will soon be green again, and just as soon
developers' machines will take great bites
out of the hill above the sea
to build new homes: for every flat a view

"equal to any in the south of France"
that village people knew, knowing no other,
and will soon belong to cannier folk.
With Italian kitchens, America's plumbing,
the proud new owners don't believe in ghosts.

FESTIVAL OF HUNGRY GHOSTS

After offerings before red doors
and smell of burning paper and bamboo,
we went home to take tea.

I fell asleep before dinner
dreaming of ghosts going hungry
for games and disputes

of children and their children
and I dreamed I stood among graves
on the hill above the village

where the newly-wakened dead,
having slept, returned among us –
and they wept.

GHOST OPERA

It's the seventh month again
and the red doors must yield.
Ghosts are bent on spreading pain.

We singers gather in a village hall
to put on make-up, costumes, wigs.
Ghosts cannot resist the call

of our music with its plangent strings,
the clashing cymbals and the gong.
We perform for all the ghosts who come.

The living villagers have gone
yet we must stay to sing of heroes, war, and tragic love,
while ghosts applaud in silence every song.

HONG KONG ROCK

It's like this:
mainly coarse grained
magical with quartz
holocrystalline twinned
with faintly pinkish felspar.

Its minerals support growth
animal, vegetable, human, economic
and canto- and anglo-
rock music rolled into seasong.

Rock sprouts through cluttered seawaves
into the cloud-pale sky
but resists no developers,
sprouts blades of glass,

The rock's a haven yet,
days already counted down
to a second liberation
and the Party's big party
echoing to canto-rock voices.

Hong Kong's a haven yet of girls
called Athena Yip or Venus Leung
up to their thighs in surf at Shek O

of girls with headsets
and couples holding hands
and men with hand-held mikes
in the karaoke lounges
of Mongkok or Aberdeen

of parties in hotels
where you hear behind thin walls
the economy's amorous cries.

116

OBSERVING THE LIZARD

On the curved tail of the road uphill
I'm at a standstill, near the gum tree grove.
I watch the ragged pages of bark
unfurled haphazardly from the trees' spines:
tattered books in nature's nursery.

Look into the twig-lace puzzle,
the tangle of slender leaves.
That strange excrescence of bark
I recognize is not hanging wood
but lizard – as if my instant invention.

The lizard clings to a smooth patch of trunk
making it ragged. He's caught, still-life,
in an arrested crawl,
back down the bark to earth,
his dusty leather-ware trunk freeze-framed,
stark still as the leafless twig of his tapered tail.

Around that slack little neck
coils a coloured frill like some wild rose;
it's a camouflage of petals
around the alert head
with its sudden stamen tongue.

I am as still, mindless for a minute, all perception.
The petals stick there like coloured questions:
are they a lizard's luck or cunning?
Sporting his tiny garland, he illustrates the woods
like a frontispiece.

OBSERVING DRAGONFLIES

I trudge uphill in morning light
toward the dragonflies.
Hundreds hover at the bend in the trail.
When I'm there with them
they turn abruptly at right angles
giving me the cold shoulder
and slide slicing away in flight.

They tack through my lines,
thought on the wing.

Verse music in my head
mixes with perception
of fuselages camouflaged
and slivers of thought-speech
melting on the tongue
and observation of a close reality:

all hover in the hot light of words.
I walk in a swarm of dragonflies.

SHANGHAI WOMAN

[for Serena Jin]

She flies above floodlit roofs
from Notre Dame to the Rugby posts
that top the Bank of China in Hong Kong.
She skims them like a woman warrior
in a film. She finds the larger goal of evening sky
above the Bund: Serena's back and in Shanghai.

Parents and shrill children pose for snaps,
delight in the restoration of the river's life,
old artery pulsing through the city.
Shanghainese chatter in the light again
as they take the promenade
above the traffic's endless flow
on the fashionable street below.

Serena listens, smiles.
She loves the accent and the tones,
discovering her own childhood's speech again,
with simultaneous interpretation
into another epoch and its meanings,
in a register never found but in the soul.

She walks beside the river
running within her deepest self
like a song from childhood.
Her most casual gesture
witnesses her style and joy.
As she walks with a lighter tread
where lights are glowing against the darkened sky,
Serena's happy in Shanghai.

China and her partners join a crazy dance,
where work and enterprise and fun
seem always on the go and never done.
Look! A moonlight woman's flying high
above a city that refused to die.
Serena's happy in Shanghai.

HOSPITAL ROUNDS

[for Dr. Nancy Leung]

Where does her compassion start?
Somewhere in the belly's pit,
like fear, or hunger, or desire?
It is no flame or fire.
Is it in the metal-tasting blood
squeezing through the pumping heart?
What merciful place can it gain
in the grey labyrinths of the brain?

Is it in the depths of her eyes,
in their cool gaze registering perception – yes
– and calculations of the odds for cure or death?
Perhaps in the professional glance, steady breath,
the necessary instruments to cut away distress,
without the anguished cries and tears.
Imagine her eyes above the sterile mask.
There is no further need to ask.

Those dark, observant eyes give her away,
when on hospital rounds she quizzes her retinue,
sharply queries a prescription's dose,
hugs someone else's granny close
and enlivens yet another disinfected day.
As we talk I think I understand.
Inside the adult self, a girl who couldn't bear
someone else's suffering still lives right there.

In the open ward a machine clanks.
Repeating its rhythm, groans from a plastic mask,
gutteral retching gasps of fear,
in a panic of gulping just to clear
the scrawny throat. She soothes the frail old girl
until her shoulders rise and fall to a normal breathing in the air.
Further down, a shriveled husk of woman sleeps in her cot
with but an hour to live through the last morphine shot.

In a separate bay, several of the middle-aged,
worn down by work and bickering,
are sitting up, expectant as children
waiting for a treat. They've already
done their hair and sit or stand to gossip.
Some smile and bow before the doctors go away.
Cured, these women will go home today.

As she steps through the double doors
with students, there's a sense of occasion,
bringing hope to the liver patient there
in the first bed. How do you measure care?
The yellow of the flesh delivers its bright shock.
At whatever age they reached before
they knew there was nothing more to do,
the vanquished dead have gone. No phantom in her retinue.

The dead do not come back.
She figures what to do for this young mother
with a blood-streaked mucous draining from her side
to a bottle on the floor. Not those who died,
but crowded wards of the living need her care.
Compassion starts and ends in living tissue
not the ghosts. Fragile ones, hanging onto life,
these claim her knowledge and her surgeon's knife.

POST OP

An orderly wheels you in
from the recovery room
awake, smiling, calm,
as if nothing has happened,
a drain from your knee
a drip to your arm...

TERRACOTTA MAIDEN

Following the customs of the palace
your gown's coral pleats drop spreading to the hem,
trail on patterned stones in the courtyard.
Your hands, palm to palm, hold your shawl
black and green around those vulnerable shoulders.

Your hair is a fold of shining black,
bird's wing above the painted composure of your face.
As women lead you to the sandalwood chamber
your eyes betray no fear.
Your name comes whispering into my mind.
Love's talons clutch and score my heart.
I have not seen you since that day.

I heard you went to some distant mansion
when your looks faded.
Spring is locked inside me.
I release your youth in this clay girl.
Tenderness pulses through my fingers and thumbs.

My lost girl, rest in the prince's tomb.
I commend you to earth's cold dark
with your peach blossom cheeks
and coral-pink gown
and the gold I put on your painted shawl.
Soon I shall follow, bent and knotted with age,
as body and soul call out for the humbling grave.

If, in a thousand years, someone carries you into the light,
the curious may notice where a thumb and finger
fashioned your hair in a favoured style.

You have returned to the light,

flaking pink and gold. Hint of apple-green.
Silent testimony of clay.
Dry reddish soil embraces you here and there.
No. Not everything is lost.

TEMPLE AT TAIPO

Between tenements blackened with damp
the narrow market street
squeezes life's flow of come and go.
Here bright-eyed children
chew sugar cane or bubble gum,
hoarse garrulous hawkers
are spreading their wares on the cement,
and a pregnant wife carries home
a fish in water in a plastic bag.

Step across limp vegetable debris
to quiet flagstones and the trees
of this little temple yard.
Step around the painted screen
that guards the entrance
to join grandmothers at worship.
In the fragrant dark
nod at that glinting goddess,
note the fortune-teller's sticks.

Touch the great bronze bell.
Inspect cracked floor tiles
peer at black rafters
under the smoke-dimmed roof.
Glance at faded, buckled photos
of fathers and uncles of the old men
now lounging on battered kitchen chairs.
Watch them slap down life's worn cards
in tricks on the plastic table top,

Drop coins in the box
as if it might augment the sum of faith
among the shadows.
Sound of the temple bell.
In the courtyard's haven
look over the wall at a tattooed youth
who argues into a mobile phone.
He clicks it closed and pockets it.
From his pocket, sound of a mobile's tune.

TURQUOISE GODDESS

They call you Guan-Yin
and expect you to bring
miraculous comfort,
when a hard life's effort
is just too much to bear.

You have been to hell and back
but the King of Death had the knack
of giving you life again.
You returned in a quiet garden,
floating with lotus plants in the pond.

Rooted in mud, the blossoms, Spring
and Autumn, spread the wings
of their petals around you,
beyond reach of the Prince of Chu.
I hold now, carved in turquoise,
admired and prized, your curves
and flowing robes, a perfect poise
amid lotus flowers, in the palm of my hand.

PARTING AT A TAVERN IN CHIN-LING

Fragrant wind-blown willow seeds float among us.
A beauty from Wu begs us taste her young wine.
Friends, you have come to say farewell in Chin-Ling.
Going, I linger. Drink up! And ask this:
River, is your East-flowing current stronger
or our thoughts at parting – which?

[Translated from Li Po by Chen Hong and Andrew Parkin.]

PART TWO

PART TWO

AUSTRALIA

AT A BEND IN THE RIVER

Frail violet stars trail their green
across red-blonde flakings of the rock
and higher, above the road, we stop
where gum trees twist pecling, silver limbs
in the subtle dance of living wood.
We listen for birds chuckling
under the trees and welcomed by wild flowers
enjoy the calm perfection of the sky.

Far below the spills and tapers
of the trees' untidiness,
the river's shallows gleam.
The lick of its huge, dark tongue
smears the pebbled curve
and all seems motionless
as time ticks away the day
like crickets hidden in the bush.

We cannot see which way the river flows.
We don't refuse the sun's embrace.
The dappled fingers of trees scratch their shadows
across the sandy backbone of the road.
Every growing thing, like a kiss,
seems planted from a vast desire
on the tanned body of the mountain.
The river slowly straightens.

It thrusts away between the rounded hills.
We follow it in silence, smiling along our route,
until we reach the strange exhilaration of the sea.

BOGONG MOTHS FOR THE PARLIAMENT

The stainless spars of pyramid and crown,
slender thrust of pole, the flapping flag:
these emblems of a nation's rule
prod the sky and focus all the town,
while coarser histrionics crowd the air
like Pandemonium's shrill cries,
and any leader could become a clown.

The hill is now a parliament
and roofed with grass the building
simulates the hill again,
as if all power knows its end,
when nature, working underground, will send
its old green fingers back to sew
a crazy drop-stitch through the concrete halls.

To government the fresh-elected go.
Men and women readily shuck off
their commonplace cocoon
and flit resplendent
on their parti-coloured wings
or simply fall asleep before a vote
that makes society a TV show.

At dusk I drive towards the hill.
My windscreen cleaves and bleeds
a sooty blizzard of the Bogong wings,
furred grub-flakes in the wipers' arcs,
as I hurtle through the swarming dark.
When Parliament switches on its lights
cleaners find every crack alive with moths to kill.

The lights extinct, moths fly on afresh
along a flight path to the coastal cave
to hang their living tapestries along the walls.
In the hills no tribal fires now hiss
with burning wings, no feast day
celebrates the season's delicate roast.
Now, moths of day, men camp near parliament and protest.

BOGONG MOTHS FOR LOVERS

After a long hot drive it's there,
the white cottage with red roof
on a slope of seaside lawn.
The soprano's aria climbs high
above the bass continuo of the tide.
Offshore the lighthouse flash
punctuates the densest text of night.

Inside we light our lamp
and lure every moth that ever lived.
The Villa-Lobos music comes to rest
in silence and a woman's lips.
I turn down the wick, blow out its flame
to make a smoky darkness grow.
We lovers watch the night's bright dome
shine above a silvered mirror.

PICTURE, GARDEN, SEA

[for John and Nina Girling]

Outside the picture you can hear
the obsessive sculpture of the sea,
with its underhand embraces for cliffs.

He stops at nothing.
The chiseled face and torso
of the shoreline must endure

his whetstone tool, his tongue's rough edge,
long licks and the sudden bites
of his frenzied, foam-filled mouth.

Smooth eye-sockets testify
to his watery gougings
with flecked fingers drilling the rock.

Amethyst declivities near knotted joints
of blonde sandy limbs
he annoints with transparencies of warmth,

blesses and adorns with Neptune's necklaces.
With sponges he swabs dappled hollows
and sanguineous fingers of the sea-borne dead.

Outside the picture too
grows a garden of sunlit lawn
where quiet breeds ideas, sheltered by bushes.

I seek the arbour of the twisted eucalypt,
where I read and muse in the feathered light
of the green afternoon of the self.

Three parrots raid the larder of a bush
holding its berries in curved beaks.
Their cashew nut tongues are black.

Here is a manner of living,
perception an adventure among friends
watching the quiet mystery of things.

Inside the picture I plunge
into Meissner's vision
of pre-history enduring engraved.

Brown rocks poke through salt-spray rags.
Red rocks bleed with ceaseless floggings by waves.
Rock is a massive shoulder and arm.

Its hand with granite fingers plunges
beneath a hem of white lace afloat
on the flared blue-green skirts.

Inside the picture I plunge
into the salt water of another's mood.
I open my eyes to etched minutiae.

As I stand dripping sunlight
I carry picture, garden, sea within me,
They do not escape. I go inside.

MARINA

In the dream of my sailboat youth
I am suddenly here on a curved rock-shelf slope,
where I stand gazing at the sea,
eyes twin pools of blue.

Drawn softly like dream thoughts
to a wall where they sleep a little
with heads tucked in motionless,
the gulls sense now they must scatter

from the tide swell slope, wave slapped,
where I cling motionless,
wind talons tugging my feathering hair
and stinging cheeks and eyes.

Gulls may bob like toys in a tub
but red stains the hook of the beak
which will open for frantic screams
as sudden as their flight to the boats.

I ride a dream thermal of images,
glide between thought long felt and words
foam flecked as my salt lips
until I land on my hands and knees on the rock

in the dream of my sailboat youth,
suddenly here between sky and sea,
balancing on sea weed festoons
and happy as a child on the beach.

It is time to dive under waves blood warm
amid gulls' aggrieved shrieks that fade
as I trail bubbles and then surface grinning,
and shake my head awake in a tropic dawn.

MELTED ICE

In the beginning of
our new-found words and time,
in a moment of intense stillness
atop the hills of winter,
you smile with delight
and pick up some ice.

You hold it melting in your hand.
I open your fingers.
Gleam of clear water on your skin.

We understood all
in that moment.
on the mountain
breathing our plumes
of hot breath into the cold.
We make no prison of the past.

Everything that follows
will be a dance of living moods
and in my dreams
or moments of quiet memory
of ourselves together,
I insist on those few first seconds.

TROUT STREAM

[for Chris and Gini Hole]

Breezy unseen fingers ripple the water's skin,
a tickle to snatch her secret chuckles out
into the gasp of words. Her crooked grin
and icy clarity approve the fatal wit
of solitary angler, fish's reflex guile.

Her creatures learn the accurate ready abouts
and tacks of stream's descent into shallows.
Further down, earth tones stipple sleek bed-stones
of river-race in Brindabella's shadows,
natural mosaic of rinsed and polished grace.

Beneath a fallen tree the sharp-toothed
jack or hen dawdle near Quince Tree Rapid
or slink to Upper Shifting Sands. Fish flow, flick back,
break cover to kill what rests, soothed
unwary by the dark in Boulton's Deep.

Berinda's grass curves to the Glide at Camper's Flat,
where waters rub like a restless cat
around his waders as he casts for trout,
rainbow or the brown. He skims from the wrist
meticulous disguises of the hook:

Snowy Mountain Hopper's black and yellow fly,
or scarlets Royal, Coachman, Wulff,
the elegantly lethal Teal and Red,
all bound with fingers deft with thread
and feather, and the artist's water-colour brush.

Patience, craft, the strike's explosion
at the lure's bright sting; relief to rod:
these are virtue at dawn's first light.
As the catch smokes, it hooks our appetite.
I haul on my line, like time, the water's rush and flight.

THE CRANES

[for Neville Quarry]

The Tatlin monument abstracts
Marxist ironies of curving time
and aspirations space attracts.
Its mechanism's struts and spars
curl in spirals like a gene
preserved from a Titan's extinct world,
while Lenin's will gleams everywhere.
It cranes its angled neck at skies
whose clouds in shreds drift past the stars.

Old Edo makes up like a whore
as Tokyo within her urban sprawl
displays at dusk her neon calligraphic face.
The rectangles, the stilts of houses,
sculptured concrete, clip-on modules
with punctured metal giving shade –
all severities of business lust lie dormant
in the pause before the morning starts again.
The geisha milks the men her art arouses.

In the latest century of pain
brought to term with labour
of the modern to be born,
accelerators set Japan's new pace
and Russian history's forgotten
as it's made. The cranes swing slow
their metal chopsticks in time's hand
to grip each day a rising sun.
Architecture is the make-up on a culture's face.

AUSTRALIAN LIGHT

1

[for Robin and Virginia Wallace-Crabbe]

Morning is leaving traces of light-fingered prints
on the brown chest; that white smudge is gloss
at the edge of a drawer.

Near the shadowed planks, the yellow door,
dim gold, glows just there
where thick walls are angled

and slope away from the pane.
Light paints the cream white
below the shadow of something unseen.

Outside in the pale blue shine of dawn
there's a small rose cloud like a faint cry
from a bird's pink throat.

Later, in warm mid-morning light
you put some of your work against the wall
and I see straight away

a different farmhouse present from other days
startled by your paint. I hold art paper
textured with creamy pores

where you printed this artist's proof
of the garden, signed, but untitled.
Grinning you pencil it: "Françoise's Australia".

Her eyes blink and salt light
stings her with joy.
You are hugging laughter.

And four of us are suddenly happy
as the sun floods across the floor
promising intense colour

for Virginia's shoot before the rain arrives.

Moments of light will become a gaiety of flowers
fixed in a dark-room tray.

2

[for John and Kerry Campbell]

The noon light sharpens everything around us
as Kerry brings from the house
coffee and cream with cups agleam
and all colours fresh as the aroma.

A concentration of dusted brown
slides near your feet.
The lizard flicks on its way under the boards
out of the light of the sun.

Light gleams in the blond streaks of your hair.
Missing John, I fancy I hear the thunder
in bursts from his polo pony's hooves
and then the clack of wood.

We delight in these same skills and concentration
in northern Chinese court ladies
as they play in the old painting
hung on the wall in Hong Kong

in a room where Kerry slept once
and where the light is different.
We conjure noon on your farm with the old fig tree
as we sit in French light, Sancerre in our glasses.

3

[for Bruce]

We arrive trailing a dust cloud,
car's brownish tail feathers spreading through azure light,
where your land stretches
itself, purring in the warmth.

And away from the dam's brown velvet eye
the deserted shed sheared away a century
to reach into a distant bleating of fleeced sheep
in the mind's keen ears.

The settler's simple house lets sky
leak through the roof over the two rooms
of the family that settled, grew, and left.
We cook our sausages.

I glance down to the dam
as you talk on the phone.
Jack, your dog, brown and white, bolts
through grass, pale olive,

hounding a springing rabbit, very spruce,
grey and white, as neat as a paint job,
all ears and tail, in a zigzag chase.
They dip into shadow and vanish.

I look at the place in this light:
you found it and appraised it all
with a countryman's observant eyes
and under the tin roof

with but the two rooms
you decide on a new veranda for shade.
The place is re-made in that contemplation
in companionable light – and it's home.

MINOU

You are sitting on a few house bricks
under the wall where the roses bloom.

Minou, your black and white cat,
stretches one hind leg

then the other, and then he purrs.
I wriggle my toe in his fur.

Each time I touch him across the years,
I'm reaching out for you.

AT ULURU

"Saturday, July 19th. Spinifex Sandhills.
Barometer 28.12 Wind south-east..." [1873]

1

"What was my astonishment to find
one immense rock
rising abruptly from the plain...
I have named this
Ayers Rock, after Sir Henry...
I left the camels here
and after scrambling two miles
barefooted, over sharp rocks,
succeeded in reaching the summit."

2

[Thursday, April 27th. 1989]

Dawn. Fresh wind brings tears.
The low-slung chain steadies us
as we climb red-handed to the ledge,
our lungs raw, ears pink
on rock curves and cusps rusted
and rutted black over millennia.
The chain draws us above earth,
above cloud shawl.

On the knobby pate all climbers laugh.
Now nearer the sky
we sign the dew-drenched book:
"Climbed Ayers Rock".

3

Black-backed hands daubed
emu tracks in a creek and
"Snakes, very cleverly done…
two hearts joined."
Images endure in a tourist mind.

4

Rock a molar rooted
deep as a mine.

Desert a rare green
surprising as rain,
silver silken
as inside skin
of earth's ragged pelt.

Rock hard centre of red earth womb.

5

The way down
rosy with sun.
Crevices sprout grass like
underarm hair.

A shadow points like a dark finger
towards the perfect ring
of a mid-air rainbow,
coloured circle of refracted light,
promise of a mystic marriage.

6

Rock ingot cooled from nearer earth's core.
Morning's blush before
day's deeper red, summer heat.

7

Heat throb of spirit's anvil,
desert rock now black
at sundown's aperitif.

8

Fertility in its rain pools and springs.
Earth's scrotum.
At dark it's the still earth heart,
hard heart, half dug out
of ancient dying sternum.

Fertile with love's sorcery,
rock dwarfs motels of modern times,
stands in a magic circle
aloof from wizards of tourism.

The climbing chain cannot tether it.
Rock held tight still.
Old grinder in earth's livid gum.

[The words in italics come from *Report & Diary of Mr. W.C. Gosse's Central & Western Exploring Expedition.*]

THE GHOST GUMS OF ALBERT NAMAJIRA

Tourists visit twin ghost gums
because he painted them as twins
when they really were identical.

You could have lined them up
by standing in a certain place
and two trees would have seemed as one.

You could have bought his visions then
for forty bucks. But now he's famous
and tourists come to take their snaps

climbing down from buses in the heat
in the middle of nowhere to learn
the trees were knocked about

when a motorist went astray.
Now the branches blacken as they die.
Namajira took a walkabout

as wide and unexpected as his land.
He finished with an alcoholic's stagger
into a jail that killed him

well before he died. Twin ghosts
stand immaculate, tangled in water-colour,
never photographed, never jailed.

IN THE LILAC SILENCE

In the lilac silence
your lips return to the mind's cave.

A rock slab's painted with memories
of ancient hunters in the bush.

Love has her hunters,
lets the prey sometimes spring away.

From nest-thickened branches
of a spinney of circumstance

I hear choruses from a past
I lived without fear.

In the mind's cave, your lips
paint crimson bows on a cold rock face.

NEW TWIN

You are my new twin
mirrored in the shining dream,
this other life, another hemisphere.

We do not brood on dreams
in the tangled nest.
We live unraveling realities.

In my head, one summer's day:
at earth's end we find each other,
each unremarkable enough, yet best.

We trace paths through the maze
to where we met, like the two hemispheres
of cultured pearls, crossing oceans.

I find you again near a wall
where the roses climb,
where you teach me how to live.

I remember a birdsong day.
On a warm slab of rock a lizard poses.
A stream chuckles along the stone-strewn bed.

Under the vast Australian sky
lyre birds dance in bush glades
and a kookaburra chortles coarsely and long.

Trees are incurious witnesses
of the small pool where we make love,
baptised again, and wed.

AT GLENLYLE

[for Dinny and Darrel Killen]

The hills roll over in the heat
like the old red setter in a road dry enough to crack.

We take a narrow track, cross the cattle-grid,
and marvel, as we climb, at grass still green.

The drive curls to the house above the dam.
Here art and husbandry find lost relationships.

Fragrance of lavender adds to the smiles of welcome.
In the cool we talk of children, business, politics.

A tapestry reminds the connoisseur of death
in hand-embroidered medieval French.

Even as we eat and talk of Russian cups and take
another glass of golden wine, I know this lunch is life

and that its memory will mellow and increase
the sense of well-being it's essential to have had.

Three acres here are planted with new vines
calmly absorbing the brutal onslaught of the sun.

The house, the farm, the friends who value intellect and art –
all celebrate the love that might heal the ravaged heart.

ARALUEN

[for John and Kerry Campbell]

At every season, every year, chipped gray rocks
bare the teeth that push through turf
where small-headed sheep move as they graze
in the clarity of southern light.

The Braidwood road flicks and twists around
for its slow digression through steep brush,
where the old strong-room for local gold
retains dark timbers now in silence, stone-thick.

I gaze through your white, arched windows
at the valley's widening smile,
that disarray of distant hills smudged blue
and a lone eagle's glide in a slow arc.

A pregnant goddess chose this valley once as home.
Her outcrop arms shelter Araluen; her thighs
are rich pastures, her thousand breasts the peach trees,
her hair the gleaming trellis of the night.

Mid-morning, by the creek, the slow hot cattle
raise enormous heads from the water's song.
Ants swarm at the ankles of an iron gate.
A horned skull bleaches, fur still clings, an ear's intact.

All logic is unstable as the drifting clouds.
Yet the farm's informal gardens always offer herbs,
drawing subtle flavour from the soil,
and there's a tree where ripening figs hang warm.

The farm and house inherit a local, settled past.
They still demand tough work, constancy, and care.
Your books and art adorn the walls.
Friendship grows rooted here with roses and the vine.

154

RIPOLIN ON HARDBOARD

[Homage to Sidney Nolan]

It's peasant armour alright:
fifty-five kilos of plough shares
snaffled from bleached huts
of stranded loneliness.
Steel plates embrace his chest
held by the bolts and nuts.

His sister softens
that helmet box –
dark oven for a head –
padding it with cloth.
The metal rusted long before
his desperado sweat and wrath.

"I am a widow's son, outlawed,"
he said, "and my orders
must be obeyed. I'm a Kelly.
They call me Ned."

They race to ride him down
on the Wombat ranges.
From Mansfield near a dribbling creek
where the Broken River crawls
to Yarrawonga's nests up north
he's on the wallaby, avoiding brawls.

He scuttles to Euroka on the tracks
and cuts across to Tallangatta's trees.
An iron flap shields his groin
but chafes his thighs. No document
offers mercy to the man unmoved
by ballads of crime and men of law.

Under the pitiless blank
of the hack-sawn eyeslit,
Nolan's skylit gap aslant,
his hard-hearted breastplate hangs
like a sign: shoot here.
In the wide silence armour clangs.

He vanishes like water
in the Glenrowan bush
and pulls its tough scrim
of terrain around him.
He camps like a nomad
as the light grows dim.

Plod through the desert's stench
of twisted carcasses, looking like cacti,
bones for spines, rotting ligaments
where maggots perform
a slow castration. On the heat's vast rack
a dead beast's hide shrinks to a mocking form.

The sun that never weeps
beats a renegade tattoo.
Kelly's hazel eyes stare red,
sometimes painted blue. Rain
is what he needs. He turns the horse,
ignores the whistling train.

Its smoke dissolves across the bridge
and the rails' long ladder on the earth.
Nolan paints the laconic scene
of Kelly's capture.
There were men doing a job.
No excess, please, no rapture.

Torn from his yabby shell he listens
as fingers and thumb of justice tug
at his head and neck.
But he wears another armour, wit.

His deviant tongue flicks dry words
at sentencing. Mentally, he'll spit.
"May the Lord
have mercy on your soul,"
says the judge in his black cap.
"Yis, I'll meet you there."
After the lethal trap
they plastered his face.

Death's hardened mask
was a last sleek armour.
Litres of ripolin dry
in streaks of energy and distress.
Sprung from history's jail, he rides
red landscapes of legend, his true mistress.

A PORTRAIT OF CHARLES THE BOLD FOUND UNDER A LATER PAINTING

[for Bettina Jessel, restorer of paintings]

That beggar's skin, cracked like paint,
a battle-hardened enemy,
steel-clad death slicing through Lorraine:
nothing brought you such dismay
as this modern woman peeling through
the *fête galante* to fix your presence.
No dream revealed the likes of her.

She lifts the veils of dirt.
Your now lustrous eye
outstares five vanished centuries
and promises a master's image
on this slab of oak.

An impossible future
brushes you with fingers
deft as your lutenist's
and unvarnishes a hundred years.
She strips blue silk gentilities
painted with a neo-classic charm
while terror daubed all France with blood.

A camouflage of wigs and postures
slides from you, dark Lord of Burgundy;
taffetas and lap-dogs slink
from the cold glint of armour.
You elbow powdered elegance aside.

EUROPE AGAIN

AT LA CHARITÉ-SUR-LOIRE

[for Nicolas and Françoise]

This afternoon rain races
across slates, darkens ramparts,
sweats on old doors and gates.

It stampedes across the river
with invisible hooves of a herd
rushing for reeds and willows.

The bridge wades up to its knees in water.
Its arches are patient horses
led at last to drink.

I, too, am patient, wait for the man
wading near the brink of the sand bank
to cast an optimistic line.

Camouflaged by weed and rock,
I become the sinuous fish.
I watch from grey-green shallows

as clouds sponge the sky blue
and sun breaks through
as in the water's flow I'm reborn.

In the gasping air,
in the middle of France
I recognize what Jeannisson sketched

then quietly, with a master's touch, engraved,
before he printed his copies and added
deft subtleties of colour.

And for me, everything, even the very old, is new.

CLOS MARIN

In my *clos marin* old walls wrap themselves
in shawls of ivy, the leaves ruffled
by sparrows and a fresh sea breeze.
On the house with white shutters and doors
sun's glitter kindles the window-panes.
I stand, a hint of salt on my lips,
breathing seaweed and mollusc-scented air
under the Conqueror's wide sky.

It's then I savour a sip of Calvados,
glimpse in golden depths the ripened fruit
of a crop more than thirty autumns past.
You close your eyes, with apple blossom lids,
and I lift my head to the sun's warmth,
the better to recall the huge rust-brown cows
swinging their de-horned heads,
slow-motion compass pointers,
towards us at the gate where they crowd;
the better to picture the ruins of Crèvecoeur,
the intimate wooden intricacies of its dove-cote;
the better to conjure dark-moated Château Grandchamp
and that demesne in the valley, La Roque Baignard;
the better to revisit St. Julien le Faucon.

In an instant all this Norman coast country froths
like crushed apples in the still of my *clos marin*
festive with periwinkle, bluebells, and the spry primrose;
bubbles with cow parsley at the edge of spinneys,
on land soaked with the blood of warriors
who charged from the ships to beach and cliff,
who floated from gliders like blossom shaken to the fiery earth.

At quayside in his brine-battered trawler
a fisherman repairs the bewildering net.
His rough red fingers ply a needle yellow as blackbird's beak,
springy-tough as the rib of a fish.
I hear shrill, savage plaints from gulls tossed in the wind.
Others float, rocked always, in mind's mirror,
nature's toys riding the waters of La Vie.

I MISS THE SOUNDS OF MORNING

In the rigmarole of my half-sleeping self
I miss the sounds of morning,
in the misty light outside
thinned to this almost dark
in a room almost asleep.

I miss the casual clatter
of breakfast dishes and spoons
or hoarse shouts of early workmen
across yards where a radio voice seems urgent.
I miss song-burst from windows or doors.

When I travel without you
I miss your voice surfacing
from waves of sleep, from dream ripples.
When you ask me the time
I hear the voice of the child you once were.

COURTYARD OF THE GOLDEN STAR

Blue light rinses these tawny walls.
Honeysuckle breathes near that door.

The shadows of the years slip away
over the worn stones of the yard.

Green eyes, weep only for happy times
of the intimate afternoons.

Under the ever-changing but indifferent sky
take my fingers again into yours.

You are my golden star.
You rise with the moon

in Paris evenings where light always lingers
over the chatter of generations before nightfall.

INNER COURTYARD

Behind a neo-classical façade
old trees heave their sighs
above the paved inner yard
as if to warn their visitors
of some unspecified distress.

Their branches semaphore
a growing panic ungrasped as yet
by residents behind the windows.
I feel a change in the air.
The pigeons are hiding somewhere.

We stepped in from the outside world
of old posters flapping gap-toothed smiles,
added monocles, mustachios,
and marginalia. Spent politicians
seem but moultards. Then they preen again.

In the courtyard a delivery man
bemoans the death of quality,
nods in sympathy with a craftsman
facing ruin by the flood of foreign, moulded trash
that swamps big stores and sinks all charm.

Here in the yard, generations of craftsmen stay.
They lived and worked, discovering sensitivities
of eyes and hands, fashioning each day
a taste to please discerning buyers
who could pay enough to make a living wage.

And now each day of global change
erodes some cornerstone of craft.
Where are the apprentices of patience,
of authentic needs, of elegant luxuries?
Where are the middle-rich, willing to buy the rare?

ARTS AND CRAFTS

Smell of the fresh-planed wood.
Tap, tap of mallet on metal tools.
Blonde curls blown to the floor.
Concentration of the living craftsman
achieving subtleties of craft
through sensitivities of hand and eye.
This energy and life are more
than value added to a tree.

Tee shirt patched by sweat,
the cabinet-maker appraises, narrow-eyed,
the wood's newly fashioned elegance.
It awaits the polisher's oil,
absorbs that patient worship,
displays all patterned grain
to the finisher's lingering caress.

THE FOUNTAIN

This shadowed entry through an arch of stone
leads us from the world's calamities.

Sunlight crystals flicker through an arc of spray.
Splashes from jets darken the encircling stones.

Eyes that saw beyond appearances have long since
closed. Now children's voices echo here at play.

Not yet for them the love or art that Sand and Chopin found
when they were here – so short a stay.

Hesitant music floats across the court.
Someone picks through a score as if a scent were lost

and then picked up again. On the dark screen
inside my eyelids, she's at her window:

she ponders and listens as Chopin works;
they both take up their pens,

create a different history to enrich
our indiscreet companion, time.

Art's jets curve beyond, behind,
across the continuous fountain spray.

SHADOWS OF MORNING

The voice of the shadows of morning
whispers across the inner court
along the swaying branches.

The voice opens like an eye
focused on one sound.
The voice closes a silent lid.

This silence is unexplained.
And without rhyme or reason
sharp birdsong unstitches

a seam of silence frayed by blackbirds
and the low murmurs of nodding pigeons.

I need no pursuit of the ideal,
nor insistence that all is vain,
no bias against bounty or beauty.

I desire no absence of this tree,
no refusal to favour the bird, the song,
in the pursuit of clever abstraction.

I find all my privilege
in this simple, cracked sill,
with geraniums, a few snapped stems,

their scent on your fingers still.

WOMAN ASLEEP

There's this faint line of light
sketched freestyle
washcd by the fine hair
of dawn's grey-dipped brush;
it shows around the roofs,
the darkened trees, and every bush.

The birds are signalling;
within the courtyard nothing stirs.

You are oblivious and relaxed,
sleek boat at anchor
riding the swell of sleep's calmer moods.
I cherish the fine lines of your face
against the white foam of sheets.

Later, you're the long boulevard,
the famous city, nearby woods.

You are the land itself,
stretched across earth's curve,
your back turned to the wall of the north,
one arm flung towards England,
thigh deep in the quilt of Italy and Spain,
your head on the white bolster of the Alps.

You summer of flowers here again,
woman asleep, you word-free song!

I touch the loops of your hair
and trace the firm ridge of spine,
worship the length of your legs
and hold you, waking and blessed--

inside us this dawn-
song of birds.

DOUBLE HELIX

Underfoot a double winding stair
fashioned long ago
by European master masons –
it exists in a few examples,
the steps concave and shiny
with centuries of climbers:
loaded genomes making for the top.

This other coded double stair,
internal miracle of interlocking blocks,
mere trace of something
tissue-smooth, commands the cells
to grow each double being and its crop:

animal and soul; he and she –
starting from necessity
yet writhing to be free.

AT THE BIBLIOTHÈQUE NATIONALE

[for Yves Bonnefoy]

In the quiet stateroom of the library,
where marble floor and gilded décor
confront our present with the calm
encoded power of time's intensities,
this statue of Voltaire, that bust of Aragon,
and, yes, the Poussin, Moses
saved among the reeds,
survive into our newest century.

In this austere, official place
where masters of that other culture
walked and breathed the witty air
of new ideas, fresh violence,
your books and manuscripts,
your trails of favoured words
trekking the fallen snowfields of the page
were laid out for inspection or an idle glance.

Here are the traces of the self-bound thoughts,
the moods of that acculturated heart
surviving France's fall and philosophical despair
that all but killed the obscure joy of presences.
You took a *rue traversière*,
noted humble thresholds, cracking paint,
and gave us the labour of your vision
glowing under lamplight as you toiled.

You find a different sensitivity for your words,
another landscape, another country lane, another role,
a place where your thought's arrows fall,
where presences shed still a healing warmth
in the chill places of the emptied soul.

THE GARDEN

Star vault above walls of the high garden,
fruit in the distant tree, but stones
of the mortal place carried in tree's foam
were perhaps a shadow from the prow, a memory.

Stars and the chalkchips of a simple lane,
you faded, deprived us of the true garden,
every pathway of starry sky casting shadow
across this shipwrecked song, across our uncertain route.

[This poem by Yves Bonnefoy was translated by Andrew Parkin and Françoise Lentsch.]

IN THE 12TH

The old rail track is now a garden
long as a green giant's arm
to stretch from the big torso
of the Vincennes forest at Porte Dorée
as green fingers reach
above the viaduct towards Bastille.

Roses scent the air and signal
different colours to old windows
where trains once rattled by.
On the grass where a castle stood
girls and lovers uncover
pale bodies in a rendez-vous with the sun.

Nerval was mad in the rue de Picpus.
Vallerand's clinic was his writer's lair.
He could find your lineage in the nails
of your fingers and toes.
Jean Falp's façades in rue Dorian show faces
with art nouveau smiles and waving hair.

In amputated Courteline's small green Square
his impassive bust faces the apartment
where all inspiration fled.
In search of wine I saunter past the magic
No.9, rue Fabre d'Eglantine, Loblee's neo-Gothic place.
Above the door an alchemist ponders mysteries with his cat.

In greenest Paris I imagine forest and marsh
and rough-hewn boats docking at Bercy.
I leap into pre-history at the Nation.

GUILLAUME APOLLINAIRE MOTORS ALONG THE AVENUE DE ST. MANDÉ

To celebrate his "modern" dawn
poet and motor car perform an air.
O antique motor of Apollinaire!
O gauntlets, goggles, klaxon horn!

I see with scarcely opened eyes
glossed beginnings of those world-war times
in old fiacres, steaming dung, new-fangled motor cars,
drugged girls who sell their flesh to faceless men.

Past and present swarm with future years
along a poet's avenue of open wounds
offered like mouths to speak our fears.
Apollinaire sings to me of old and new

and shouts across the engine's roar,
the merits of a dusky whore, of trepanned head,
of death, the no-man's-land,
of shell-shocked relics from impending wars.

St. Mandé's courtyards shade their jazz-age loves,
where now the needles and discarded condoms lie.
Courteline dies near Picpus, before the second war,
and martyrs of resistance fall near nuns and doves.

I crave rough intercourse of history and myth
in morning sunlight of the Paris June.

Look! A paper dart from a nineteen-nineties hand
dips towards old buttoned leather ware,
comes gliding through another century to land,
and rides that rattling motor with Apollinaire.

LENIN'S PARIS PRESS

A morning paper to be read
while we sip the hot black coffee
and chew our daily bread:

a newsprint Lenin takes the air
(that cap on his head)
in Maria's loving care.

Proud Herr Doktor Ochs
stands ready near the chair
and (with knowing looks)

plays to camera and comrades
before the future's lens and books.
The fanatic he parades

for photographic lies
smiles from a face bereft of sense,
and rots before he dies.

His syphilitic brain
acknowledges no duty, no offence,
weighs no loss, no gain.

That historic brow registers more pain
and conjures real or fancied plots.
Groans cram the rhetorician's throat in vain.

DEATH AT GORKI

In sluggish hours
before dawn's light,
howls of agony proclaim
the lowest point of Lenin's night.

This is his last assault on fame
amid the Gorki peasants,
weary of statistics, dogma,
and his very name.

No state-paid thugs dare drag him from his bed.
Life's intimate disease, though, turns the screws,
even if he is Top Red
and recovers all the Party's dues.

THE LEGACY

Peasants who resist imperatives of change
like orchard fruit in rows are strung
from boughs they climbed when they were young.

It's over now? Worshippers are blind
to the Gulag of his rotting hide,
the merciless sclerosis of his kind.

The Party couldn't simply let him die,
so his mummy mocks the curious
with a propagandist's lie.

Corruption incorruptible
reposes tombless and on view
to voyeuristic strangers in the shuffling human queue.

The grand-children of Bolsheviks
have seen another chaos come.
And they carry Russia's future, kicking in the womb.

WELL BEING

At the open window with geraniums
across from the great paulownia
busy with morning sparrows,
we sit with our wine.

Bubbles support the fine mousse
as it vanishes, tickling air.

A lunch-time sun
kindles our glasses,
traps itself in a stream of bubbles,
and makes the world more fun.

This is no fantasy or fuss.
Wine's nose and quaff and finish
are part of it, and simple friendship,
and reality's scattered crust

stalked by sparrow and dove —
these are wisdom enough.

ARC ACROSS TIME

Framed photographs of the dead
as they gather in the sepia of time past
watch me from hooks on the wall.

They are tight-lipped
as if they had never spoken,
nor would ever, nor recall

childhood. But what did parents say
to their parents, to god-parents,
to uncles, aunts, and friends?

What rapid words made them smile
as they struck that pose
after the christening?

Their animation I don't doubt,
nor that burst of laughter
they send me, as I listen

for echoes of traces on an arc across time.
Backs to the wall, they fade further each day
behind modern glass edged with passe-partout.

Who was that man at the wedding
in dress uniform, with an empty sleeve?
What other sacrifices had they made for France?

I know the codes of their alien language,
received as a gift of fragments from all and sundry.
But what are these bland looks, those nuances?

Leafing through an album, smiling, I recognise
them next at a wedding party, and register the pain
of someone who cut away the head of a man in spats.

ARC ACROSS CULTURES

We sense the attraction,
find another person
we can love
and, if it works enough,
we may share a bed
and we may even wed,
so when we mix our blood
we may create some good
new bright beauties
from two families
two cultures and two races
or more, further back,
for which there are new places
in hearts and minds more spacious.

We create the fresh, audacious
someone, not easily a bore,
for this new person grows
knowing and loving more
than just one family,
however extended, or
more than one village, one city
one language, one country,
and never just one, exclusive, haughty race.

These children can be champions and win
their share, whatever race they're in.

THE WEE J.B.

In the rue du Rendez-vous
we sit for a morning coffee
where the pigeons swell and strut:

rou roucoule rou
roucoule rou roucoule
from a ruffled pigeon throat.

At the crossroads
neighbours of all ages throng
under a Van Gogh sun.

With the narrow blade
of my Perry & Co.'s pearl-handled Wee J.B.
I cut the pages of another book.

Should I slice further
than the portion that I begin to read
or all to the chapter's end?

Fragments of books are shrapnel
stuck in the mind. In the drained cup,
I ponder the crazed glaze loved by Chinese potters.

Involuntary rendez-vous with parents long dead.
My father peels an apple, skin one green curl,
proffers a slice, balanced on the Wee's blade.

Mother's reading the adventures of Colonel Bramble
with the aid of a trusty Harraps. When she died
the books were open at her bedside.

I pay the bill and leave
to find warm daily bread.
Walking home we chew on a crust.

181

LOVE AT DAWN

Morning's here once more,
like a young man home at last
in the early hours
from someone else's bed.

I bless the calm farewell of night.
A neighbour kicks a motor bike alive
and rolls along the empty boulevard
a giant's roaring severed head.

We've broken one another's chains.

In the narrow bed we now connive
at cheating time: your voice
arouses in me all the hard
commands of passion, till it's fled.

I open shutters peeling paint.
Warm hands of summer caress my face,
feather light. The great paulownia
is in flower, the sky tinged red.

TRACES

Yes, Caravaggio saw it
or even played his part,
recording it for some patron
and his folk to see
before newspapers
and television took their place:
that naked executioner
sweats at his work…
a child is running
and howls as he flees in horror.
And the condemned,
finally mute as the canvas,
was once yet twitching,
and then, like a model, still.

PLACE DU TRÔNE RENVERSÉ: THE OFFICIAL LIST

First Voice:

This is the official list
in which I read the names
of thirteen hundred and six
the condemned and guillotined
from the 26th. prairial
through the 9th. thermidor
of the year two
put down meticulously
by the revolutionary tribunal
of the Paris Commune
not far from here
at the Place du Trône-Renversé.

Second Voice:

No matter what their age or sex
they lie in the strange disarray
of group gropes in two mass graves,
neighbours and strangers linked
with heads rolled from their trunks
planting their red, random kisses awry.
Bodies were stripped before the sprinkled lime,
Their garments laundered for resale.

First Voice:

Statistics stubborn as teeth
fixed in a soiled skull:
eleven hundred and nine were male;
one hundred and ninety-seven female;
among these unfortunates
five hundred and seventy-nine
were men of the people,
one hundred and seventy-eight military men,
one hundred and thirty-six "gens de robe",
one hundred and eight were clergy,
one hundred and eight were noblemen,
one hundred and twenty-three women of the people,
fifty-one were noblewomen,
twenty-three were nuns.

Second Voice:

Of course, there were some writers.
André de Chénier, son of Greece and France,
praised the revolution,
condemned the terror,
wrote his Odes and Iambes
in custody at Saint-Lazare,
mounted the scaffold at what's now the Nation.
He loved wisdom and died for truth
two days before the fall of Robespierre.

He served the Muses.

Third Voice:

Is it fascination
with the workings of the fatal toy
more than bloodlust
that drives them to destroy
so many, even the very old?

First Voice:

The oldest in the batch
is that dangerous counsellor
of the Parlement at Toulouse,
Jacques Bardy. He's eighty-five.
How come a man so old is still alive?

Second Voice:

Among the youngest, Joseph Vérine,
Number 1271, is sweet sixteen
like the hairdresser of the same age
who also walks the blood-drenched stage.

Of those who die at seventeen
is Number 1129, de Saint-Pern,
who's made to learn his lesson
at the cutting edge, poor lad,
because we couldn't find his dad.

First Voice:

Well, well, here's a boy sailor
with his teenage wife;
their deaths will rescue them –
from knowing all the strife
of married life.
And – why not? –
let's add this adolescent jockey,
Hugue Hot!

Second Voice:

Ah yes, Number 791,
young Adelaïde Liénard,
we'll dispatch together
with her widowed mother.
Neither'll need to mourn the other.

Third Voice:

Why bring them back again?
They all lie dumped in the nuns' garden,
rue de Picpus. Just beyond old La Fayette
and the young American looking at the Stars and Stripes.
They didn't die to make a better world.
They didn't die for us.

In the year of our glory,
two hundred-and-whatever,
let's just say, as we board a jet,
we still know about victims
and just as easily forget.

HISTORY'S OFFICIAL LISTS

The official lists historians compile
Note of course the acknowledged great and famous,
often vile, who always flower
into the exercise of power.

This being said,
I'd rather bow my head
to victims of that power instead.

CODA TO THE OFFICIAL LISTS

First Voice:

They're always getting in the way
so the masses have to pay
with their taxes and their blood
because it's only for their good.

Second Voice:

Getting in the way of what?

First Voice:

Ideas, dogma, plans, the way ahead.

Third Voice:

And that's enough
to let officials
get so tough?
De Sade was in the rue de Charenton.
He was safe but not the Nation.

ANNE FRANK HAUS

Searching for No. 263
in the narrow street
alongside the canal,
I hear the church bell
strike the hour nearby –
as she must have done.

I carry an overnight bag –
heavy enough
to make me weary.
But I persevere
and find her address –
as they must have done.

Tourists queue there now,
some out of curiosity
about that secret home,
some perhaps hoping to grasp
an understanding of that girl
God would not protect.

A goods train leaves the station
clattering north-east, as she did.
I take the Paris train.
I see horses in a field,
and half a mile of lavender
like an unexpected tribute.

No wreath, in a claustrophobic heap
on a slab, trying to keep her fresh
in the mind. The field's not funereal
but growing and alive with a purple wave.
From behind the hurtling glass I imagine I scent it –
pungent here, though vanished into absence.

LEIDEN

A few sheep in the meadow,
three dark chestnut horses
lying on their sides,
and two fat swans on the riverbank
are waiting for rain.

If I could paint, I'd show them
under this sagging sky next to a house.
I'd hang my picture near a water-colour
of a black canal flanked by reddish houses
three hundred years old.

In my picture, though, Van Gogh,
through a window like an inset, top right,
would lean out to survey his handiwork
opened like an advent calendar
at other windows.

Gauguin, at yet another window,
bottom left, looking up
at his old friend, and grinning,
would point to all the doors
and shutters daubed with tropical beauties.

Great lotus flowers would float
with window-box orchids reflected
in the watery lane of the canal.

AFTER THE STORM

Ride a cock horse
to Banbury Cross...

After the autumn storm
a wood pigeon hoots
huskily its reassurances
for a quarter of an hour
in the growing light of dawn
and then is silent.

I'm six again: woods around the house
at Marston St. Lawrence
in Hitler's war of nineteen thirty-nine.
Smell of damp earth at the roots of trees.
Wind among the green and silver leaves.
The tethered goat munches fallen conkers.

Adult now, curious to revisit
the childhood scene *en route*
for another destination,
I climb again the uphill lane
that curves among cottages
and pass the strange, half-remembered rectory.

The white horse gallops
across the paved yard of my mind,
riderless and loud. Weeping,
too young boarder I once was,
I brake near the hedge. No bells,
nor eternal joys among old oaks and elms.

I turn over in my Paris bed.
Is that a pigeon's feathery call?
Is it from now or then –
added by war to these happier ears,
to that old rhyme now well-remembered,
which trots for no reason jingling back?

CAPTIVE MIND

Captive mind, squeeze through the bars
of cages of dogma
and leave behind broken chains
of kamikaze blandishments.

Leave the tin plate of prison fare
worm-eaten with class hatreds
and soar above air-lanes of terror
seeking brighter stars than bitterness.

TWO ENVOYS

[for Robert Desnos]

1

A shadow among the other shadows
he sang his own last song
to a love still at large in the sun.

2

Go now, celebrate this life
beyond all death camps,
in the teeth of the skulls in their heaps.

FREEDOM

We have all but succumbed to evil times
of tyrannies and plagues and wars
so hard to survive that human kind
might think that time itself
would flare and end in a roar of flame.

Would there have been and still might be
the four last trumpets' notes defying
all that went before to fade to silence?
But like a sudden blossom "the time is free"
after a tyrant's fall.

Let crowds in the streets dare to hope,
dare to think, and utter that word "freedom"
in any tongue and in voices hoarse
with today's boundless spirit,
though cracked by families of pain.

MORNING IN PARIS

In dove-gray morning coats
as they pick their way across the grass
swelling tawny breasts, with a hint of indophane,
nodding as if to clinch a point,
or let one pass, like shoppers in a store,
the pigeons forage in the morning light.

Awakened perhaps by the dawn chorus
of the smaller birds, I suppose
pigeons are sentinels of the parapet,
guards assigned to the base of a conifer,
and some spies to send breathy call signs
across the inner court. But silent they seek.

And after his sweetest song
the blackbird's yellow beak
becomes the scissors
to cut and mince
some cringing creature,
caught in the midst of its smaller world

where it hangs twitching, as if at birth,
or suddenly still after the snatch from damp earth.
Indoors, I watch through a window-pane, as in childhood,
the dog at my feet, lying low
in soft-muzzled sleep, tail slowly awag
in the toils of a sharp-scented dream.

Remembering a distant Australian dawn,
I feel again the cat's inconsiderate paws
as it stalks with tail's slow lash
across human hillocks
of master and mistress,
half-conscious in bed's embrace.

Church bells toll me back to Paris,
to Brazilian coffee and brochettes,
and diagonal slices of baguette.

WARM BREAD

We have broken the bread of life again
Warm from the baker's shop
And again you have poured coffee and juice
In the slanting light of the courtyard.

With these gifts, quite plain,
you have given your smile,
the words that fall towards silence,
petals blowing loose.

In the grey-green light of your eyes
I read our world of trust
and cut from life's well-worn pack
our favoured cards, like slices from the loaf.

WEDDING SONGS

1

The shrill voices of birds
greet us from secret places
behind the leaves of the spreading tree.

Everywhere today we encounter
clouds and wings
of feathered angels

who have always hovered,
unseen, unknown, in a golden light,
gods and goddesses of plenty.

Is it they or our secret selves
who led us, after so many years,
into one another's arms?

2

We have returned,
it seems, from some high adventure
to greet old places as friends.

Echoes of younger voices,
unwitting, repeat patterns of living
in the narrow streets.

The fountain in the square
plays the eternal return
of water to stone.

Look! Martlets rapidly sketch
freedom on the vast blue cloth
stretched above the orange tiles of roofs.

By the grace of a warmer sun,
our lives flourish again,
in the plenty of almond and olive.

CHOREOGRAPHIES

Quietly absorbed near the window
I watch the paulownia wave
its green wings, their feathers
sprouting each side of the leaf stem.
They signal me, unhurried,
in the tree's hesitant dance.

It is best to move with the slow rhythms
like the sheltered birds.

I dance, swaying arms and trunk
to follow the tree's moves,
celebrate for another year
a clean bill of health.

Have we lived too long
beneath irradiated clouds?

Soon, as before, I shall take off
from the golden statues and bridges,
from a world of blonde stone
cleaned of chemical wear-and-tear.

I shall leap east or west
into the troubled future.

EVENING WALK IN UMBRIA

We walk in golden light

between the lane's old briars and squat trees.
A smile of recognition flashes as you pluck

a soft green plum.

I take another from the cluttered branch
and, as I bite, warm juice spurts

between the teeth,

too much it seems for one small mirabelle.
From swaying branches we pick again

popping them whole this time,

amazed by so much sweetness crammed
in as small and delicate a thing.

Busybody birds swoop

across the lane as I look beyond the river
to cattle grazing on the plain.

We do not talk.

This obscure path of summer led us
to a rich moment of content

in which we seem

discoverers of life – yet tread old earth
where countless others, before and after,

may once have known,
and yet may know, the same.

RHYME

Hey diddle diddle
the cat had a riddle:
Queen Nut jumped over the moon.
The dark hound god laughed
to see such sport
and the fish
swam out of the tomb.

BONAPARTE'S *DESCRIPTION*

["L'Egypte fut le théâtre de sa gloire." – Fourier.]

He broods, the way actors do. He juts the lower lip.
This is the grand invasion of another space and time
by something later, a modern France, ready to advance
its long dalliance with Africa.

The Emperor's imagination's all but spent,
gratified by Sphynx and Gizeh's pyramids.
In bloodshot eyes of sunsets over baking sand
he foresees no Russian winter.

His scholars re-invent an Egypt
in the copious *Description*, writing down one land,
its sinking monuments, sediments of cultures,
in the discourse of another.

Lieutenant Bouchard finds the Rosetta,
stone code book, that would have gone to France
but the British win.
Napoleon decamps from Alexandria.

The ink is dried by sand on nineteen years
of writing and research. Twenty-three tomes
become his monument, a gift to scholars.
Hamilton completes *Aegyptiaca.*

The ancients made a cult of death.
Moderns perfect all instruments of war.
Archaeologists dig and brush through debris.
King Tut with golden toys awaited Carter.

THE DENIS FRESCOES

In the moted light of the church
frescoes by Maurice Denis arrest the visitor.
He left his mark also in the Theatre
of the Champs-Elysées, the Petit Palais,
and the palace of Catherine de Médicis
now the home of the Senate.

He paid homage to religious art
and to Cézanne, making us look
with modern eyes, see flat surface,
patterns of colour, yet still
he's there in the picture
with the Nine, a book in his lap.

As colours and forms of looming trees
and of muses seeking different lovers
gather dust and fade, his head remains
favoured in the foreground
with two majestic women lost in each other
and from whom he has looked away.

ONE WAY STREET

The headlong thoroughfare
streaks like a river
through the rocky gorge of buildings
from the source at Carrefour Netter
to the great lake of the square.

I make no rendez-vous with politics.
Does it make a rendez-vous with me?

Pillars, stone angels, and the kings,
the houses of the Barrière remain,
eroded witnesses carved by artist-masons.
The seventy pound blade fell in blood slicked grooves.
Heads rolled like flasks of wine near a drunkard's cart.

The grandeur of a surge of energy
strides from chaos towards another square:
Dalou's "Triumph of the Republic".
As I turn at last to join the crowd
there's his "Candour"

its ontology is the head of a girl
looking from the window of a car.

The open square, the Nation,
and its tributary streets,
the famous sculptor facing the future,
monuments of kings looking to Vincennes,
two histories and the living girl, perpetual sensation,

and this game of *boules*, its loungers
looking on at rolling spheres,

unrelenting traffic, human mystery
under ever-restless, constant sky –
all seem equal in the vivid scene.
I make for the rue du Rendez-vous,
and find it empty, or as full, as politics.

MUSE

*"I know the years, and what coarse entertainment
they afford poetry."* Henry Vaughan.

1

You never deserted the great Florentine in exile
but gave him vengeful powers of satire
and of rhyme to mock the cruel and the vile.

The rapid crackle of his words on fire,
the Portinari girl come back to overturn his life,
and *terza rima* glinting through the medieval mire!

Yes, he was human: a man who had a wife,
children, work. No palace for a mistress;
satire his weapon, not the knife.

From the dark of life's distress
Andrea's austere fresco shows a learned man –
hollow-cheeked *gravitas* – step into light's caress.

His life's moderate span
ended in Ravenna's quiet tomb.
From wide-eyed saints began

his spiral back to spirit's secret room.
Florence. Immortal love. God. Humiliation. Pride.
What else was there to find, what else presume?

He left his sacred poem's worth implied.
It finds its lodgings way beyond the frontiers of time.
His vision's heaven mounts above earth's sins, accused and tried.

The poem is our pilgrimage and shrine.
The poem is his country's generous spring,
the sweet new style as graceful as sublime.

204

2

At school I read the great sonnet
about sailors mocking the bird
brought down with its mangled wings.
It was then you beckoned me
but I was no boy wonder.

I glimpsed you once in Asia
not far from Huangkong Beach.
I was too preoccupied with Russia
to appreciate the hint.

I fell among scholars.
Yet you returned to me in the north
dancing through blizzards,
and broke me open
to put the words of men and women
in verses on my lips.

3

You were the Egyptian girl
who opened my sleep-filled eyes
and embraced me with angel's wings.

You were a sliver from an old willow,
little carved swimmer,
like a splinter in my soul.

As Kuchuk Hanem you knew the lust
of calculating, self-conscious Flaubert:
"effect" of your necklace between his teeth.

4

In the eternal city
you sit in Nero's golden house
amid the rubble of history,
devious desecrations of time,
centuries of abuse, robbing you
of your face, a knee, an arm.

Yet your white stone gleams
under an artful placing of light.
The sculptor didn't give you wings.
You were a slender girl,
diaphanous robe gathered by ribbon
under young breasts.

Did vandals mock you, reveling in the harm
when they sliced away your face?
What did they do with your arm?
Where is the golden flute,
where the seven-stringed lyre,
where the petal-soft foot?

Beauty can score
and sere the heart
in the gloom of ruins.
You are old Grecian stone
left broken on a dusty floor.
Yet you live in the halogen light!

5

You are with me now,
on a dirt road in the hills,
in an Australian winter,
taking fresh snow in your hand
letting it melt in your palm,
trickle through your fingers,
drops of the sweetest moments of life.

6

In Paris you favour
this tree in early June
where pigeons rest.

Their breathy voices
bring me to the window-box.
Side by side, we listen.

That great leafy presence
seems the entirety of life
in a small courtyard.

You are so close now
I could kiss your silvered nails,
smell snapped geraniums there.

In vaulted cellars
you keep two thousand poets
for living eyes and lips to read.

You are Bonnefoy's figurehead
slipping through the swell
of unfathomed lines.

Behind the mask,
the painted face
and histrionic eyes

you preserve form and phrase,
expressive periods,
where passion stalks.

You let passions ambush actors
in the Palais Royal cafés,
even as they talk.

And even as you guard tradition
you welcome those who make it new.
You have pierced tongue and lip

and encrusted the curved rim of one ear
with pearls on a golden pin.
You come and go at will. Abused, you always win.

7

In a window, a jade slab shines,
moonlit, on this autumn night.
Carved in relief on the hard stone, dancers.

In the traffic's turbulence
I wait for green. Your face in repose
attains beauty's solemn concentration

of living bone and flesh.
I watch you signal,
arm raised, slim hand turned,

gesture from another land.
You are no antique statue
but a woman vivid and alive.

At the crossing's green
we meet; your arm slips
through mine, your slender hand

rests on mine. Like spilled blood
your lips gleam as you murmur,
"Where are you going?"

"I shall say farewell
to Asia for a while, but not to you."
"Where are you going?"

How can I foresee pathways
through time? Europe calls.
Canada beckons. England hails me.

Gesture from another land,
no antique statue now,
but Pacific woman, vivid and alive,

you have posed your question,
put coals on my tongue,
made the harbour turbulent.

I have no answer for you.
Out of the sea will arise
the shipwrecked self and all its words.

8

On a beach near Shizuoka
a Frenchwoman danced
for the fisherman in *Hagoromo*.

Her shrine on the beach
brings Umewaka's company
and their feathered robe.

Your smile plays on lips
of the masked girl standing apart
unseen in evening shadow.

Sun gleams on Fuji
as cloud curtains part
and her snows turn rosy gold.

9

[For Rosalía de Castro]

On the mountain, an artist's chiseled granite
commemorates writers born on the great peninsula's edge.
Mist rolls its veils around the heart's intimate abyss.
Wild horses stamp the grass and canter away
through clouds swathing a place weighted with myth,
cradle of bones from the unencumbered dead,
born down here, where bird-thronged estuaries
mix fresh water with salt tides of the sea.

Dawn. Quiet grove of oaks. You led us
to rough-hewn rocks delicate in equipoise.
The Dolmen's art endures like crags. Graffito.

Through her villa's sun-filtering windows
Rosalía smiles at figs she planted
with olive, lemon, grape.
Words burst across her tongue
all the juice of life.
Emotions leap and cling, surprising
as wild flowers pushing intensities of colour
between weathered rocks on the wind-disheveled shore.

Rose petals fall
one by one
from Rosalía's
generous lips.

In the village bar across the way
flies buzz the hand of one who paints
that now familiar face
and her farewell to life,
learned by heart in local speech.
Poet, your clothes hang empty and cold in your room
but your words are warm and filled with your presence.
I take them with me, like the gift of a friend.

ON THE MOUNTAIN

[for Deanna Lee Rudgard]

Sudden twistings of the mountain's trails,
each dogmatic slab of damp rock face,
stubborn weathered outcrops,
where meagre, clinging grasses root,
despite the pointless wailing of the wind,
are like thought's perplexities.
Ideas suffer their erosion, or the drop
into the void of deep crevasses.

On ribbon roads so far below
the mountaineer, unthinking worldlings
ignore a new thought's stubborn routes,
ignore old questions that once could goad us
to climb again the trails and veer
to even higher fastnesses
for a broader vista underfoot,
yet still imperfect, partial vision.

And then the sun bursts through the haze
like a revelation of the land below,
lit, though not entirely clear
of drifting shadows' beauty and derision,
ambivalence in thought's sheer face.
The climber, testing the handhold of a new approach,
gulps down air and grasps another rock to seek
the lonely splendour of a cloud-entangled peak.

CUMBRAE FLAMENCA

Darkness of Galician night
amplifies the singers and guitars.
The wall, as in a sacred cave,
glows with a rose-pink light
and echoes voices roughened by life's scars.
Smack of hand on hand,
Slap of flesh on wood, on hide.

Commended by the calloused hands,
a dancer flounces near the torches' flames
and strikes a pose of human pride;
her shadow grows from where she stands,
looms as darker goddess, gypsy bride.
Clack and snap of wood on wood.
Flame intensifies the lightning of the eyes.

Obsessive music's turbulence and fire
urge the woman to display what now she signifies:
the prize of sensual love and beauty traced
in a dancer's pathways of desire
that lead to grief as cruel as the love that dies.
Sudden thunder of the chords.
Smack of hand on calloused hand.

The dancer stamps, glares, tight-reins a secret life.
Slow serpents of the arms and hands.
Hair's black feather falls across her brow.
Passion on passion mounts the arch of back, the thresh of thighs.
Heels stamp that bitter anguish of desire –
thud of flesh on wood, steel clacks as fast as heels allow
when she quickens to a climax like a fire!

VELAZQUEZ IN THE MIRROR

Velazquez is reflected as he paints.
Now we are the mirror,
facing the room at court.
Millions of eyes,
some idly scanning,
others severe, intent,
some professional,
create in this other room
the world's mirror of generations.

The court's exclusive craft
left us the teasing image
of diminished king and queen
presented in the painting's glass
next to an open door
and someone pausing
in the knowing light
never to enter
nor yet to leave.

We confront the posed Infanta,
favoured dog, the dwarf.
Velazquez looks beyond
his set square loom of canvas
drying paint, poised passion of wet brush,
slightly to the side
of what he hides.
Master of this moment, lover of candled night,
he faces himself, the mirror of judgment,
back turned on imaged monarchs
even as he paints them in.

In an eternal present smelling of oils
he discovers the mystery of things real,
the polished, shadowy court,
the plain back of his canvas stretched on its frame.

VICTORY AT SAMOTHRACE

Was it the head
they smashed up first
in that riotous Aegean dawn?
Did it roll
and was blood shed
because of some tyrant's thirst
for power? Trails of bubbles
burst near the creaking hulls.

That one-winged figure,
missing head and arms,
still has purpose and a stride.
She needs no plaster wing
to assert her vigour
in a museum's calm.
The Kabeiroi lost shrine
and goddess but not their pride.

We moderns found a marble palm
and certain fingers.
History cannot record
all the fingers broken, one by one.
A severed arm
in art's history lingers
for it once made
a triumphant sign.

Torn from the shoulder too
in the frenzy of that time
which victors left for silt
and sand and centuries to cover,
did the other arm give a clue,
make a sign for something more sublime?
Was a culture of the mind and heart
half-remembered, handed on?

From Hiroshima's flash
our history blasts off
and change, the shuttle,
accelerates, pressing us back
through life. Now we have to dash
just to keep on track.
We may lose our one blue bauble
in the star-bright mesh.

Not dogma nor idea explains an age.
Class warfare's futile as a racist rage.
Our freedoms need compassion's head and arms
embracing ever-shifting facts and time's alarms.
But somewhere under tall Fengari's care
a severed head grows sponge for hair.
A smile or half-smile curves still on a face
beneath the splash-down sea off Samothrace.

ON A PAINTING BY CLAUDE: COAST VIEW, THE ORIGIN OF CORAL

Near the dark hoof of eroded cliff
planted up to the ankle in foam
miracle arrives on the beach:
as Perseus rinses blood away,
the white horse spreads wings
and Gorgan's head makes coral on the sand.

What cries are choked
when coral sprouts along the throat?

In this painted light, figures from myth
form their triangle of different concerns.
Off the coast a disk of moon,
concentration of what never drowns,
shines through the gentle waves.
Your brush strokes light along the shore.

What cries are choked
when coral sprouts along the throat?

You lay horizon's level calm
across the agitation of the sea.
That tough stone-rooted tree
thrusts at a tranquil sky
contingent realities of leaves.
Are the birds about to sing?

What cries are choked
when coral sprouts along the throat?

218

Your image of relief from dread
centres in this tangle of weed,
a nest for the Gorgon's head,
where coral is forever made –
your hero's back being turned –
branched miracle of the dead.

DEVIL'S CHAPEL, ST. WOLFGANG

In the heart of God perhaps,
as here in His house,
Mephistopheles waits in all weathers
to wither the hearts
of those who have despaired.

Will they be delivered from this devil
whose statue spindle-twists
through pliant souls, if they descend
a few steps to keep faith
in the bright baroque world?

Ahead of us the pulpit soars.
To right, the gold of inexplicable soul,
its complexities embodied here
in crafts that defeat echoing sermons
and surprise us like music from aloft.

This church with its devil's chapel,
raised a little to the side,
surprises us with contradictions
in the hearts of all, priests, people, God.
It's the double pulsing heart of poetry in stone.

CARYATIDS

We have counted on them for support,
female and eternal, since the perfect posture
of those Ionic women of white stone
made almost flesh showed us the way
beyond the mere male column.

Bookish Goujon,
sculptor to the king,
modeled the firm-breasted girls
of ancient Athens,
robes knotted at their navels –

we don't doubt they exist
hidden in their stone bellies
like knots in oak –
who still support, despite their severed arms,
the Tribune of Musicians in the Louvre.

Models of his last plain style,
an austere Attic purity.

Here in Austria
the caryatids uphold values
in a close order of model matrons,
polished marble or a more granular surface,
features fixed in a smile or frown.

Their necks and shoulders ache
and behind the blank eyes
in their stone skulls
the urge to escape grows
with the desire to let drop

the entire weight of centuries
behind them as they walk,
only a column of air above them now,
stone guests coming to the feast,
the sunlight casting their shadows.

One day they will find the way
to step down from the plinths,
like Hermione at last,
and – however briefly – live,
their stone made flesh.

PART THREE

SHARDS

1

Fragments held up to the light
piece by piece, examined scrupulously,
suggest the complete picture.
It existed once.

2

Shards could mislead,
seduce the mind's eye,
leading it beyond the jagged edge,
persuading the imagination
that a country and a culture
could just once have been whole –
or that restorers might glue it
leaving hair-line scars.

3

There was no completion
only change,
only the ragged orphan history
growing up unwitting and never mature,
moving on from each generation of victims.

4

Maybe I invent splinters of memory
in the never finished city
in a country
trying to glue itself
together again.

5

Fractured villages,
dividing waters,
sampans splitting the air
with oily motors, all this
making untold obscure lives sting.

6

Splinters of life sting,
slide unexpected
under the skin
when a mirror cracks.
On each side of a frontier
people's lives mirror
the others until one day
a mirror shatters
bit by bit.

7

Before they blinded me
out at sea, the only law the boatman,
there was always sky,
clouded and close,
air pungent and humid,
never far from the slap of waves,
then as now, and the cries of gulls.

8

Sampans creak and rock
smelling of seaweed and sweat
as anonymous men
slide like splinters
into the flesh of blinded whores.

9

Perhaps I invent
large red-brown cockroaches,
reed mats, creaking timbers,
beery breath, my cry like a gull
on the wing on high,
and grunts of brief satisfaction.

10

Perhaps I invent
another country,
another city,
more than a city,
concrete spread like topping
across a slice of spongy land.

11

Villages stick in the folds of valleys.
Jagged edged, they chafe and sting
their disinherited women.

12

The pride of accomplished women,
inheriting only the subordinate position,
is a whale bone stiffener, as in a garment.
They feel it with every move they make.

13

What was lost
may be found;
words dredged
from the harbour's mud.

14

Fragments of porcelain:
glazed image of a woman
at a moon gate with peaches.

15

Fishermen near a broken bridge
in porcelain that gleams faintly,
set with its curve in the lid
of a lady's polished wooden box.

16

On a shard
I admire a face
crazed by time's secret glaze.

17

In the box
she has put letters,
bark shards burned white
by life's flame.

18

On the green chequered cloth
you have put daisies
in an old yoghurt pot,
their white petals tinged red
as if you had kissed them.

19

Your steady breathing
in the shuttered room
reassures me
as the silent moon
rides its varnished sea.

20

Early birds signal
for a good half hour
before pigeons swell on the roofs
cooling in the air,
strut on chimney stacks,
and launch their husky voices
above the tree's slow dance.

21

Daisies have been shaken out
across the lawn's green cloth
like salt soaking up a little wine.

22

Ivy hangs its dark tapestry
over the old brick wall
and in its thick weave
you can see light-green stars
of the new growth.

23

In this other country
that is incomplete,
in this other city…

24

Maybe I invent
these shards of memory
to mutilate history
and the little histories that cling.

25

Your head is flung back
below the curve of your neck
and your hair falls free of the bed
and shines like water.

26

In these hills
I catch the sound of a gong
coming out of the mist.

27

Moored in a quiet bay
sampans rock,
memories sway,
and someone empties the sea
of swimmers with one shout:
"Sea snake!"

28

Smugglers roar for the dark line
of the Chinese coast,
their four outboards lifting the prow
churning waves like cream,
as they tow something heavy
that surfaces and sinks,
surfaces and sinks.

29

Shenzhen collects fragments of China
in the park of the 57 cultures,
while the university has a small
nuclear physics lab.
and through the window on the world
you can see the Eiffel Tower
puncture the sky.

30

In Szechuan House
steam hisses from
the curved copper spout
a metre long of the tea kettle.

31

We drank tea by the river in Nanjing
where candidates freed from the cages
of the Imperial Examination Centre
celebrated their success
in the days of the Qing.
We sang the jasmine tea song.

32

In a special luxury park
Mao and other leaders stayed
for holidays.
At the foot of the steps to the monument
to Sun Yat Sen, a crowd of security men
surrounds a Japanese delegation.
The retired leader bows, eyebrows
still beetling and badger grey.
The rape of Nanjing is not fiction.
It is more than memory.

33

Old earth is rich in ruin,
mud of the Pearl River,
and sunlight sends needle-thin beams
into dingy flats of artists and writers
dredging their ragged images and words,
and the People's Liberation Army
commands fresh water pearls to sell.

34

golden city of sunlight on stone
no longer new and unreal
city of spiralled districts
shells broken by time
circling the Seine

35

China awakened from nightmares,
her fragmented beauty reflected
in the cracked mirrors of peasant bath houses,
she performs her elaborate ritual
of beauty again in Shanghai and Suzhou
with their French trees in avenues.

36

In Guangzhou the restaurant offers
a banquet for forty-eight persons
who may dine on the donkey
tethered outside next to the menu,
and content with his nose bag.

37

At the mosque you can hear
the call of the Muezzin
but the handful of worshippers
do not know his language.

38

In the revolutionary barracks
where Nationalists and Communists
took lectures and learned to shoot
the old photographs fade and grow mould marks.
There's Trotsky, Lenin, and old Marx!

39

We watched the fisherman
with the tethered bird
scanning the river
amid the crazy mountains
and grottoes of Guilin.

40

"We are all broken," she said.
"All of us? When?" I asked.
She did not answer
but looked at the glazed
shine on the pool
of the Master of Nets.

41

I thought she was smiling
because of the curve of her lips,
the bunched cheeks.

42

"In childhood,"
she added, eventually.
Her voice shook.

43

Fifty-five years ago
my grandfather held my hand.
I remember silver hair
but not his hand.
It was the day before he died
peacefully in his sleep.

44

Things get broken by accident
as well.

45

Shards of the self
get cemented back
in a different order.

46

"Let's stick together."
"Yes," she says,
"bits of us."
"I think I can imagine
the whole picture."
She holds me tight.
Is it enough?

By the same author

Poetry

Dancers in a Web
Yokohama Days, Kyoto Nights
Hong Kong Poems
(with Laurence Wong)
From the Bluest Part of the Harbour
(edited anthology)

Prose

The Dramatic Imagination of W.B. Yeats

Drama Editions

Stage One: A Canadian Scenebook
Dion Boucicault: Selected Plays
W.B. Yeats, The Herne's Egg
Shakespeare Global/Local
The Hong Kong Imaginary in Transcultural Production
(with K.K. Tam and Terry Yip)

239

ANGLO-AMERIKANISCHE STUDIEN - ANGLO-AMERICAN STUDIES

Herausgegeben von
Rüdiger Ahrens (Würzburg) und Kevin Cope (Baton Rouge)